INTERMEDIATE 2 AND HIGHER
HISTORY
Course Notes, Book 1

The Growth of Nationalism in Germany, 1815–1939

Appeasement and the Road to War, 1933–1939

✕ John A Kerr ✕

Text © 2002 John A. Kerr
Design and layout © Leckie & Leckie
Cover image © Reuters Picture Archive

10/280107

ISBN 978-1-898890-98-0

Published by
Leckie & Leckie Ltd, 3rd Floor, 4 Queen Street, Edinburgh EH2 1JE
tel. 0131 220 6831   fax. 0131 225 9987
enquiries@leckieandleckie.co.uk   www.leckieandleckie.co.uk

Special thanks to
Alexander Burgess (sub-editing), Cathy Sprent (cover design) and Finola Stack (illustrations)

for Jack Oscar Kerr, the future in the past

A CIP Catalogue record for this book is available from the British Library.

Leckie & Leckie Ltd is a division of Huveaux plc.

Leckie & Leckie has made every effort to trace all copyright holders. If any have been inadvertently overlooked, we will be pleased to make the necessary arrangements. We would like to thank the following for their permission to reproduce their material:

- Punch Ltd for the cartoon 'The Goose Step' by EH Shepard, originally published in *Punch* in March 1936 (p 75). Thanks also to the Political Cartoon Society for supplying this image;
- *The Courier*, Dundee for an extract from the *Dundee Courier and Advertiser*, 9th March 1936 (p 77);
- Solo Syndication / Associated Newspapers for the cartoons 'Increasing Pressure' and 'What's Czechoslovakia to me Anyway?' by David Low, originally published in *The Evening Standard* on 18th February 1938 and 18th July 1938 respectively (pp 85 & 90). Thanks also to the Political Cartoon Society for supplying these images.

Check it out!

You may find the occasional word that is difficult to understand. How about looking it up in a dictionary or asking your teacher? Don't pretend you know what something means when you don't; you will only miss out on something important.

Other World Events in . . .

We have included a series of yellow boxes that tell you what else was happening in the world at the same time as the key events that you have to learn. The information in these boxes is not part of the syllabus, but is for your developing interest in history. Think of all the other ways of life and events that developed during the periods you are studying. It's a bit like watching the news and learning what else is going on besides the big stories!

Contents

Introduction

Knowledge of the past provides an essential guide towards understanding the world we live in today. That is particularly true concerning developments in the twentieth century which have, most immediately, shaped the conditions of the present. Amongst the more significant events of the last century was undoubtedly the Second World War. Understanding the causes of that global conflict – and the unsuccessful attempts to avoid it – not only throws light on many of the important social and political issues of the mid-twentieth century, but also introduces the excitement of historical debate. For historians do not simply record the past, they interpret the available evidence – thus giving rise to argument and controversy.

However we interpret the origins of the Second World War, there can be little dispute that Nazi Germany played a crucial role in those events. Although National Socialism was a product of the twentieth century, and the outcome of a lost war and severe economic distress, Germany itself achieved national unity in the previous century. Understanding that process, within the context of nineteenth-century Europe awakening to the idea of nationalism, provides another essential building block in our comprehension of the contemporary world. The concept of nationalism did not only take root in Germany, it became one of the dominant forces responsible for shaping the familiar world around us and continues to do so today.

But, over and above the significance of the issues covered in this volume, the study of history itself offers valuable experiences. It teaches us to collect and analyse evidence, to develop and organise our ideas, to assess and challenge interpretations, and to express our conclusions with clarity and precision. History sharpens the mind. Don't just take my word for it – think about it!

Paul Vyšný

Department of Modern History
University of St Andrews
http://www.st-andrews.ac.uk/academic/history/modhist/

University
of
St Andrews

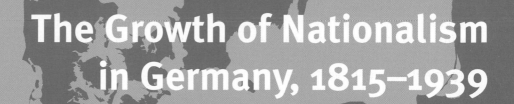

The Growth of Nationalism in Germany, 1815–1939

The Birth of Nationalism in Germany

Syllabus relevance

Intermediate 2:
>   Reasons for the growth of German Nationalism: division into states; the influence of Napoleon Bonaparte.

Higher:
>   Reasons for the growth of national consciousness in Europe in the early 19th century; reasons for the emergence of Germany as a nation state.

At a glance

In 1800, the territory which became the German Empire (1871–1918) was made up of 200 separate states. In 1806, the French Emperor, Napoleon Bonaparte, merged these German states into 38 larger states, some of which formed the Confederation of the Rhine.

The Growth of Nationalism

The main theme of this section is Nationalism, a definition of which is:
>   Nationalism is the belief that belonging to a nation is more important than belonging to a town, province, class, social group or religious group, and that the nation should do everything in its power to defend its interests and identity.

Germany and Napoleon

The creation of the Confederation of the Rhine

Before the nineteenth century, Germany as a nation had never existed. The area which was to form the German Empire in fact consisted of over 200 small states – the only states of any size or note were Prussia and Austria – which were all part of the Holy Roman Empire. In 1806, however, Napoleon dissolved the Holy Roman Empire by reorganising the German states into 38 larger ones and establishing the Confederation of the Rhine. Although the sixteen German states which made up the Confederation of the Rhine maintained some independence, they were nevertheless under the ultimate control of the French.

However, Napoleon was not trying to create a unified Germany. Instead, he was more concerned with protection against his enemies and did not believe that the weak and divided German states were adequate. Napoleon wanted the River Rhine to be a strong border against France's enemies.

How did Napoleon affect German attitudes?

In his book *Europe since Napoleon*, historian David Thomson wrote that 'the French . . . spread Liberalism by intention but created Nationalism by inadvertence.' He meant by this that the French intended to spread new political ideas such as Liberalism. However, by defeating and occupying the German states, the French united these German states in a common feeling of resentment against them.

In contrast, historian Golo Mann argued in *The History of Germany since 1789* that before 1815 there was almost no national 'German' resistance to Napoleon.

Section summary

In this section you should have learned that:
- Napoleon created a group of states, which together were called the Confederation of the Rhine;
- the Confederation of the Rhine was intended to help protect France from attack;
- some Germans started to feel a common identity because they faced a common enemy – the French.

Germany in 1815

Syllabus relevance

Intermediate 2:
> Reasons for the growth of German Nationalism: division into states, the Vienna Settlement and the rise of nationalist sentiment, the reaction of Metternich. Austro-Prussian rivalry.

Higher:
> Reasons for the growth of national consciousness in Germany.

At a glance

In 1815, the Confederation of the Rhine was replaced by the German Confederation (*Deutscher Bund*). The largest power in the German Confederation was Austria. Prince Metternich, who was the Austrian Chancellor, hoped to use the German Confederation to block any political change which could threaten the power of the old rulers. By 1848, however, economic and cultural changes were happening which challenged their power.

Why did the old rulers fear Nationalism and Liberalism?

In 1815 the Austrian Empire was the strongest European mainland power, but new ideas like Liberalism and Nationalism threatened the unity of the Austrian Empire.

- Nationalism was the desire of people with a common national identity to have their own country.
- Liberalism was the desire to have a parliament where rulers were elected by the people of the country.

The man most associated with protecting the unity of the Empire was Prince Metternich of Austria.

What was the German Confederation?

This was mainly a renamed Confederation of the Rhine, with very few changes. It was not a move towards Liberalism or national unification even if, in hindsight, it looked as if the reduction in the number of German states was heading towards the creation of fewer, but bigger, states. In fact, the German Confederation was designed to prevent too much change.

The Assembly of the German Confederation – also called the Diet – represented the rulers of the German states, not the people. The rulers in the Diet, and especially Austria, were against any changes that would weaken their authority. In fact, Article 2 of the Confederation said its main purpose was 'the maintenance of the external and internal safety of Germany and of the independence . . . of the individual German states'.

Other World Events in . . .

1815 Napoleon Bonaparte returns to France from exile on the island of Elba and begins a 'Hundred Day' rule. On June 18 he is defeated by British, Dutch and Prussian forces at the Battle of Waterloo, led by the Duke of Wellington.

The country of Switzerland is created as a confederation of 22 cantons (regions). Later this year, Switzerland's neutrality is guaranteed by seven European nations.

The cost of fighting the Napoleonic wars leads to rising unemployment, economic depression and political discontent in Britain.

The rise of Prussia

The Congress of Vienna (1815) sowed the seeds of future conflict between Austria and Prussia.

Metternich believed it was in Austria's interests to keep Germany divided and therefore easier to control. However Prussia was given more land in the centre and west of Germany as a reward for fighting Napoleon. The result was that Prussia became the biggest 'German' state. In hindsight, it is possible to see here the beginning of the rivalry between Austria and Prussia which would not be ended until Prussia defeated Austria in the war of 1866 (see pages 21–24).

Section summary

In this section you should have learned that:
- the German Confederation replaced the Confederation of the Rhine in 1815;
- Prince Metternich was Chancellor of Austria. He opposed Liberalism and Nationalism;
- by 1815 Prussia was emerging as an important force amongst the German states.

Practise your skills

In Paper 1 of the Higher course all the questions require essay answers. The purpose of this exercise is to guide you through an essay structure and revise the work you have done on Germany so far.

This is not a full-scale essay, but it introduces the importance of **relevance** and **structure** for any essay that you write. Unlike full-scale essays, this one can be quite short, perhaps just over a page long.

Practice Essay

Did the German Confederation help the move towards German unification?

Remember – topic and task!
Decide what the question is about (**the topic**) – the organisation and aims of the German Confederation created in 1815.

Decide what you have to do (**the task**) – Did the German Confederation mark a move towards German unification?

Your **introduction** must outline what you will do:
- outline the background to the situation in 'Germany' in 1815. Where had the German Confederation come from? Markers describe this as 'putting the question in its context'.
- briefly outline the two sides of the debate and why such views are held.

In the **main body** of your essay, you should demonstrate what you know about the subject:
- Describe the arguments and evidence that support the view that the German Confederation helped the move towards German unification.
- Use any evidence you have found in your own studies, for example, the fact that the number of German states had been significantly reduced, which in hindsight could perhaps be seen as a move towards unification in the long term.
- Describe the arguments and the opinions that do not support the idea expressed in the title, for example Article 2 of the German Confederation.

Make sure that you answer **the question that has been set**. In other words, make sure your answer is **relevant**.

In your **conclusion**, you should:
- refer to the main question;
- make clear what side of the argument you support;
- decide what you think is the most important and decisive piece of evidence;
- consider the use of hindsight in the debate. Patterns may be easy to recognise after an event, but when events are unfolding, they are often difficult to see.

Honesty check
If you didn't include these points do you now understand them? If not, use these gaps in your knowledge as points to revise or to ask your teacher/tutor about.

Metternich, repression and Cultural Nationalism

Syllabus relevance
Intermediate 2:
> Reasons for the growth of German Nationalism: the growth of national identity as seen in the development of the student movement and the reaction of Metternich.

Higher:
> Reasons for the growth of national consciousness in Europe in the early 19th century; reasons for the emergence of Germany as a nation state.

At a glance
After 1815, Metternich became worried about the growth of student societies, many of which supported Liberalism and Nationalism. The Karlsbad Decrees of 1819 tried to stop the spread of new ideas. At the same time, many Germans began to think in a more nationalist way and became more interested in their common culture. This was called Cultural Nationalism.

Student societies and the Karlsbad Decrees
After 1815, many students embraced nationalism and criticised Metternich's power. They moved around Germany from university to university spreading their ideas. In 1817, the conflict between Metternich and the students reached a peak at a festival in Wartburg, Saxony, when a life-sized model of Metternich was thrown onto a fire. Metternich was furious and worried. If nationalist and liberal ideas spread, Austria's power would be weakened. The result was the Karlsbad Decrees of 1819, which banned student societies and censored newspapers. The following year, the power of the Diet was increased so that soldiers could be ordered to stop the spread of new ideas in any of the German States.

Cultural Nationalism
Although Metternich had used the Karlsbad Decrees to stop political change, there was little he could do about the German poets, authors and composers, for example the Grimm brothers and Beethoven, who had begun to encourage feelings of national pride in the German states through their work. This growth in a feeling of German identity is known as 'Cultural Nationalism.'

Johann Fichte, the head of the University of Berlin from 1810 until his death in 1818, summed up the meaning of Cultural Nationalism when he argued that Germans should recognise a broad national identity, rather than view themselves as belonging to a particular region or state. Fichte was not the only person to talk about Nationalism in Germany, nor was he the first. However, his prominent position in Germany meant that his comments indicated that important changes were happening in the country at this time. He described 'Germany' as the fatherland, in which all people spoke the same language and sang the same songs. He ended by saying that freedom was the right to be German and to sort out one's own problems without interference from foreign powers.

However, you must be careful when discussing Cultural Nationalism to remember that its impact was largely limited to educated Germans and that not everyone was interested in such ideas.

Section summary
In this section you should have learned:
- that Metternich considered student societies a threat to his authority;
- what the Karlsbad Decrees were;
- that the growing popularity of German musicians and writers gave people a sense of belonging – in other words a national identity was growing;
- that this feeling of belonging was called 'Cultural Nationalism'.

Economic Nationalism and the Zollverein

Syllabus relevance

Intermediate 2:
Reasons for the growth of German Nationalism: economic development and demands for economic unity; the Zollverein; growth of Prussian power; Austro-Prussian rivalry.

Higher:
Reasons for the growth of national consciousness in Europe in the early 19th century; reasons for the emergence of Germany as a nation state.

At a glance

The Zollverein was an example of economic Nationalism because it brought German states together, excluded Austria and increased the power of Prussia.

The Zollverein

We have seen that Political Nationalism was virtually dead between 1820 and 1848, having been suppressed by the Karlsbad Decrees. You also know that Cultural Nationalism was important to some people, but that it was not vital to the everyday lives of most Germans. Economic factors were of greater importance to the story of German Nationalism before 1848. This information is summarised in the graph on the following page.

Prussia had coal and iron, vital ingredients to begin an industrial revolution. As Prussia became richer, smaller states realised they could make money by trading more freely but that trade between the different states was difficult. To encourage trade, Prussia formed a customs union in 1818. This meant that members of the union would not have to pay taxes on goods as they were transported from one member state to another. By the 1830s, this customs union was called the Zollverein.

Other World Events in the . . .

1830s In 1830, the American Congress authorises the removal of Indians from all states east of the Mississippi River.

In 1831, *The Hunchback of Notre Dame*, by French novelist Victor Hugo, is published.

In 1832, the Great Reform Act makes the first changes to British parliamentary elections for over a hundred years.

In 1835, Hans Christian Anderson publishes the first volume of his *Fairy Tales*.

In 1836, Mexico sends 3,000 soldiers to attack the Alamo, a fort in Texas. The fort is defended by 187 Texans for 13 days until it is overwhelmed.

In 1837, Queen Victoria is crowned in Westminster Abbey. She reigns until her death in 1901.

The Zollverein was very important because
- it was a major reason why Prussia became the most powerful German state;
- as Prussia's economic strength grew, she became a challenger to Austria for influence over the German states;
- it was a prototype example of what would happen later – a 'united Germany' under Prussian control that excluded Austria.

By 1836, the Zollverein included 25 German states with a total population of 26 million people. The Zollverein did not just help trade, it also helped Nationalism to spread. As trade increased, ideas spread and different German states realised that they benefited from closer contact with each other. A new railway network, centred in Prussia, also helped to bring the German states together into a single economic unit.

Why was the Zollverein so important to later unification?

Although the economic changes that the Zollverein encouraged brought the different states together, it was not originally intended to promote unification. The separate German states joined the Zollverein for their own financial and economic benefit. The Zollverein did, however, increase the power and status of Prussia.

Without the Zollverein, Prussia would not have had the muscle to defeat the power of Austria. Historian William Carr has called the Zollverein, 'The mighty lever of German unification'. Indeed, the Prussian foreign minister had said as early as 1845 that 'Unification of states through trade will eventually lead to the creation of a unified political system under our leadership.'

Austria was excluded economically from the German states long before it was excluded politically. Once Austria realised just how important the Zollverein had become, it suggested a new organisation called the Zollunion under its own control. However, the plan was rejected by the other German states, who thought that their economic future lay with Prussia.

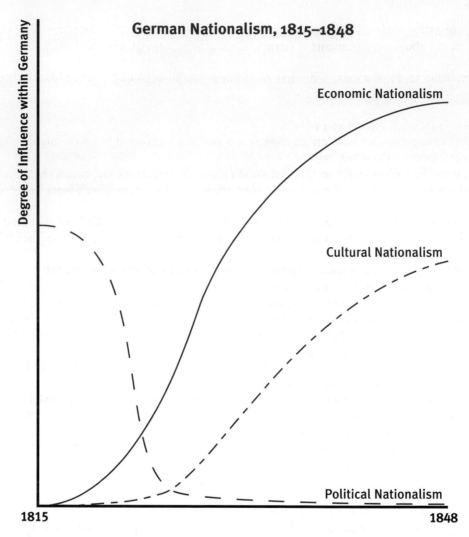

This graph is not an absolute picture of trends in German Nationalism – it simply gives an idea of some of the elements and their degree of influence.

Section summary

In this section you should have learned that:

- the Zollverein assisted moves towards unity;
- the Zollverein showed the increasing power of Prussia;
- the Zollverein has been seen as a prototype (or early version) of a Germany which excluded Austrian influence.

Practise your skills

Do you agree with Bismarck's opinion that the period between 1815 and 1848 was a time when nothing happened?

Decide what the question is about (**the topic**) – Be careful! Although the question mentions Bismarck, this essay is NOT about him. It's about developments in German Nationalism between 1815 and 1848.

Decide what you have to do (**the task**) – discuss what happened to encourage Nationalism between 1815 and 1848 and assess how important each event was.

Your **introduction** must outline what you will do.
- You have been given one opinion ('a time when nothing happened'), which might refer to political Nationalism after the Karlsbad Decrees.
- You also know that things such as Cultural Nationalism, the industrial revolution, the Zollverein and the spread of roads and railways all happened before 1848 so some things clearly were happening.

Mention these points briefly in your introduction. You will explain them more fully later. By doing this, you are showing the marker that you know what the question means and what direction your essay will take.

In the **main body** of your essay, you should demonstrate what you know about the subject:
- Is there anything to support Bismarck's point of view? Point out that with the banning of the student unions after the Karlsbad Decrees, the opportunity for Political Nationalism to grow was greatly restricted. You could argue that, politically, Austria still dominated the Diet of the German Confederation and therefore the German states, but you could then say that other types of Nationalism were growing. This provides a link to your next paragraph.
- Explain the importance of Cultural Nationalism, giving some of the ways in which it was expressed. Explain how it helped spread pride in Germany and moves towards national unity.
- Move on to Economic Nationalism. Explain how the industrial revolution changed Germany, how the Zollverein created changes that increased Prussia's power and how it helped make Germany more united.
- It is often a good idea to let a marker know that you know about historical debate by using a quotation giving the opposite point of view from the one in the title, so choose something that disagrees with Bismarck. What about using Carr's 'mighty lever' quote as a contrast?

In your **conclusion** you should:
- try to reach a balance that considers all these angles;
- think how the simple graph in this section showed three different types of Nationalism;
- suggest that German Nationalism was not just one development but that there were at least three nationalist pressures happening, albeit at different levels of importance in the years before 1848;
- mention the difference in progress between them in your conclusion;
- finally, make clear which side of the argument you support.

Honesty check
If you didn't include these points do you now understand them? If not, use these gaps in your knowledge as points to revise or to ask your teacher/tutor about.

Germany and the Revolutions of 1848

Syllabus relevance

Intermediate 2:

> 1848 – the year of revolutions in Germany; the reasons for the failure of the Frankfurt Parliament; relations between Austria and Prussia, 1849–61.

Higher:

> Reasons for the growth of national consciousness in Europe in the early 19th century; reasons for the emergence of Germany as a nation state.

At a glance

The revolutions of 1848 were important because they were the first attempt to challenge Austria's power in Germany. A new German parliament was started in Frankfurt but failed. You should know why it failed and what lessons the failure had for the future of Prussia and Germany.

The year of revolutions

Revolutions occurred in most European countries during 1848. In March of that year, demonstrations took place in Berlin and other German cities. The old rulers seemed to give in quickly to the demands of the Nationalists and Liberals, especially when they heard that Metternich had been forced to flee Vienna.

Liberal demonstrators wanted:
- freedom of speech
- freedom of the press
- political rights.

Nationalist demonstrators agreed with the liberals but they added something else to the list of demands – the creation of a united country ruled by an elected national parliament and a written constitution.

The 1848 Revolution in Prussia

In March 1848, giant demonstrations rocked Berlin, the capital of Prussia. At first, its King, Frederick William IV, tried to stop the demonstrations by force. Eventually he decided to grant the demonstrators what they wanted. Frederick William agreed that a new German parliament called a National Assembly would meet in the city of Frankfurt in May 1848. He also declared that 'Today I have taken the old German colours . . . Prussia henceforth merges into Germany.'

The 1848 revolutions – success or failure?

By the summer of 1848 it seemed as if the revolutions had succeeded:
- in many German states the old rulers had fallen from power;
- the German Confederation had crumbled;
- in Austria, Metternich had gone and Austria was distracted by revolutions within its own empire.

By 1850 it was all different:
- the National Parliament in Frankfurt had collapsed;
- Germany was not united;
- King Frederick William IV had refused to lead a united Germany;
- Austria was back in control.

Other World Events in . . .

1848 A series of revolutions spread through the Italian states, with the ultimate aim of removing Austrian influence from the country. Despite early successes, these revolutions fail.

Pope Pius IX flees Rome, returning in 1850.

Slaves on the Spanish ship *Amistad* mutiny. They kill most of the crew, seize the ship and, although attempting to return to Africa, land the ship in the American state of Connecticut.

Karl Marx and Frederich Engels publish *The Communist Manifesto*. They predict that capitalism will lead to a revolution in which the workers will take over the means of production and develop an ideal classless society.

In art, the Pre-Raphaelite Brotherhood is formed by a group of English painters, including Dante Gabriel Rossetti.

There were three main reasons why the revolutions of 1848 failed:

1. Arguments broke out within the Frankfurt Parliament
   The middle classes were happy enough to get rid of the Old Order but not when rioters attacked their property. The working classes wanted a revolution to improve their living and working conditions. They didn't think those changes were likely in a parliament controlled by the middle classes who were also their employers. The different social classes could not unite when old authority reasserted its power.

   Another argument was over the future shape of Germany. Should a unified Germany be *grossdeutsch* (including Austria) or *kleindeutsch* (excluding Austria)?

   States still friendly towards Austria and which didn't want Prussia to dominate the new Germany supported *grossdeutsch*. Supporters of *kleindeutsch* did not want to include Austria.

2. Austria and its allies in the German states had recovered
   By 1849, the Austrian army was ready to crush opposition, bring back the old rulers and restore the Austrian-controlled German Confederation. In contrast, the Frankfurt Parliament was not strong enough, either politically or militarily, to resist Austria.

3. There was a lack of strong leadership
   In the spring of 1848, Frederick William of Prussia said he would lead a united Germany. However, in March 1849 he disappointed the hopes of German Nationalists when he refused to accept the offer of the crown of Germany. Publicly, he couched his refusal in diplomatic language, stating 'the message you bring me has greatly moved me . . . but I should not justify that confidence . . . if I, violating sacred promises, were without the voluntary assent [agreement] of the crowned Princes of our Fatherland, to take a resolution [decision] which must be of great importance to them and to the states they rule.'

   Frederick William knew the German Princes would never 'voluntarily assent'. Privately, he is alleged to have described the offer from the Frankfurt Parliament as a 'crown from the gutter' and a 'crown of shame'. The Frankfurt Parliament was seriously weakened. Yet Frederick William's changing attitude is perhaps not that surprising. If he had tried to resist Austria he would have risked losing power again. In other words, he was looking out for himself.

The failure of the revolution – lessons for the future?

By the end of 1849, the Frankfurt Parliament had crumbled, the revolution was left without a leader and the hopes of Liberals and Nationalists seemed to be dying. However, Frederick William was still ambitious. He liked the idea of leading a united Germany, as long as a parliament did not control his actions. In 1849, he tried to create a different form of united assembly under his authority.

The Erfurt Union

The Erfurt Union was an assembly of German princes under Prussia's control. Prussia, which was the most powerful German state, ordered the German princes to join the Erfurt Union. By 1850, however, it was obvious that Frederick William had miscalculated. The German princes felt they had been 'bullied' into the Erfurt Union and now supported Austria as a balance against the Prussian King's ambition.

Austrian recovery

Austria was determined to destroy the Prussian challenge to its power and Schwarzenberg, the new Chancellor of Austria, said, 'we shall not let ourselves be thrown out of Germany.' He also said, 'Let Prussia be humiliated and destroyed.'

The struggle for influence between Prussia and Austria came to a head in 1850. A state called Hesse-Cassel, part of the Erfurt Union, asked for help to put down a small revolution. Austria and Prussia sent troops to help, both claiming their right to do so. For a time it looked as if war would break out between the two. The struggle grew into a showdown over who had power in the German states. At the last minute, Prussia backed down and a meeting was arranged at Olmutz which became known as the 'Humiliation of Olmutz'.

At Olmutz:
- Prussia had to agree to the cancellation of the Erfurt Union;
- Prussia had to promise never again to challenge Austria's power;
- the old German Confederation was put back in place.

When the Prussian and Austrian politicians met at Olmutz, it looked as if Prussia's chances of uniting Germany were over.

Had the revolutions achieved anything?

Later in this unit, you will discover the importance of Count Otto von Bismarck, who was to become the first Chancellor of a unified Germany and is often singularly credited with uniting the country. However, in 1848, Bismarck was opposed to the Liberals and Nationalists and saw the failure of the 1848 revolution as a lesson for the future. Bismarck became convinced that only force could decide the future of Germany.

When talking about the future of Prussia and Germany, Bismarck said that the problems would not be solved:
> 'by speeches and majority votes – that was the mistake of 1848 and 1849. Germany does not look to Prussian Liberalism for its strength but to its power.'

It would also be wrong to see Olmutz as a crushing blow to Prussia. Prussia's political ambitions were put on hold, but Prussia's real power, stemming from its economy and the Zollverein, was left untouched and it continued to grow rapidly in the 1850s. The revolutions of 1848 and '49 turned the focus onto Political Nationalism, while Economic Nationalism continued behind the scenes.

Section summary

In this section you should have learned:
- why revolutions broke out in Germany in 1848;
- why the revolutions failed;
- why Austria seemed to be back in control of the German states by 1850;
- what lessons were learned from the failure of the 1848 revolutions.

Prussia and Austria in the 1850s

Syllabus relevance

Intermediate 2:
  Relations between Austria and Prussia, 1849–61.
Higher:
  Reasons for the emergence of Germany as a nation state; the process of unification in Germany.

At a glance

In 1850, Prussian power seemed to have been destroyed, yet by 1860 Prussia had recovered and Austria had lost some of its influence.

Check the Dates! Does the question go up to 1850 or 1860?

An exam question may ask about the progress of unification up to 1850, in other words the failure of the 1848 revolutions, the continued hopes of Prussia at Erfurt and the crushing of these hopes at Olmutz. However, if the question asks about the 1850s in general a slightly different picture can be drawn.

In the previous section, you found out that in 1850 Austria seemed to have crushed Prussia at Olmutz. During the 1850s, however, a number of nationalist Prussian lawyers, teachers and businessmen formed a group that campaigned for national unification. It was called the *Nationalverein*. They said that the German Confederation should be replaced and that it was the duty of every German to support Prussia in order to achieve firm, strong government.

Clearly, hopes for unification under Prussian leadership were still alive in 1859, nine years after the Olmutz 'humiliation'. The hopes of Nationalists were not dead.

Why was Austrian power weakening in the 1850s?

Austria knew it would have to break up the Zollverein if Prussian economic strength was to be weakened. In 1852, Austria suggested making a new customs union to replace the Zollverein, but the plan collapsed.

For many years Austria had been friends with Russia. But in 1854, when Russia was at war with Britain and France and asked for help, its old ally Austria refused. Russia was furious; Austria had lost an important ally.

The image of the powerful Austrian army was weakened by a war fought against Italian nationalists (who were supported by French troops) in 1859. Two serious defeats showed that the Austrian army was not as powerful as it had once been. Reporters at the time described the Austrian army as lurching from disaster to disaster and as weak and disorganised.

Other World Events in the . . .
1850s
In 1850, Charles Dickens publishes *David Copperfield*.

In 1850, Levi Strauss invents blue jeans.

In 1854, the Royal and Ancient Club of the Old Course at St. Andrews is established to oversee the rules of golf.

On October 25, 1854, a brigade of British light cavalry is destroyed by Russian artillery as they are ordered to charge down a narrow valley in full view of the Russians. The Charge of the Light Brigade is to become the most famous incident of the Crimean War and is immortalised in a poem by Alfred, Lord Tennyson.

In 1859, Charles Darwin publishes *On the Origin of Species by Means of Natural Selection*.

By 1860, it was unlikely that German unification would take place by democratic or constitutional means. Austria would naturally resist unification since this threatened its power. Only Prussia had the strength to challenge Austria. The next few years would tell if Prussia could succeed in this challenge.

Section summary

In this section you should have learned that:
- Prussia seemed politically very weak in 1850;
- Austria seemed to be politically very strong in 1850;
- during the 1850s, events happened that weakened Austria's power and influence;
- Prussia's economic progress continued. Evidence such as the Nationalverein shows that Prussia was still seen as the future 'leader' of a united Germany.

Practise your skills

'The 1850s saw a surprising change in the balance of power between Prussia and Austria.' Discuss this view.

The **topic** of this question is the way in which Austrian power declined, while Prussian power recovered in the 1850s.

Your **task** is to explain why, in 1850, Prussia seemed unlikely to challenge Austria's power but then revived and why Austrian power declined so that by 1860 the balance of power had changed considerably.

> The above question is posed around an unattributated quotation. Don't panic! Answer the question on the basis of your factual knowledge and focus on the general issues that the quotation raises.

In your **introduction**:
- show that you understand what is meant by the balance of power;
- outline the situation in 1850 – why Prussia seemed so unlikely to revive and why Austria seemed so dominant;
- indicate some of the main reasons for the changing balance of power you will develop later, such as economic growth in Prussia and diplomatic and military problems for Austria.

In the **main body** of your essay, discuss why Austrian authority was dominant in 1850. You should certainly mention that:
- the Frankfurt Parliament had collapsed;
- the old rulers were back in power;
- the Erfurt Parliament had failed;
- Frederick William had proved to be an ineffective leader;
- the humiliation of Olmutz demonstrated the strength of Austria.

But, make sure you present the reasons why Prussia recovered:
- Prussia's economic power was greater than Austria's;
- Prussia was increasingly seen as the powerhouse and centre of any future German state;
- the *Nationalverein* showed that Prussia was still at the centre of continuing nationalist hopes.

Try to show that although Austrian power was declining, it was still a powerful state. Reasons for this decline would include:
- the *kleindeutsch/grossdeutsch* debate indicated increasing discontent with Austrian influence in Germany;
- the diplomatic split with Russia lost Austria an important friend;
- military difficulties in Italy suggested a state in trouble;
- Austria lacked the resources to develop economically.

In your **conclusion** you should make clear what side of the argument you support.
- State whether or not you accept the presented point of view and briefly summarise your own argument. You might want to pick on the word 'surprising' as this highlights the unexpected direction that events took.
- Casual observers in the 1850s might have thought that Austria would be the major force in German politics for the foreseeable future, but it was clear that power was shifting to Prussia. But be careful. Austria was still in charge of the German Confederation. Its power over the German states would not be broken until defeat in a war with Prussia in 1866.
- Your final point could be that, by 1860, there were signs of a changing balance of power, but the change had not yet happened.

> ## Honesty check
> If you didn't include these points do you now understand them? If not, use these gaps in your knowledge as points to revise or to ask your teacher/tutor about.

Bismarck and the Dispute with the Landtag

Syllabus relevance
Intermediate 2:
   Bismarck's appointment as Minister-President; relations with the parliament and the military.
Higher:
   Reasons for the emergence of Germany as a nation state.

At a glance
Bismarck led Prussia into three wars between 1864 and 1871, which helped to unite Germany. Before Bismarck began his campaign to unite Germany, he had to make sure of his authority (on behalf of the King) over the Prussian government and its army. Bismarck's political attitudes were shown in the way he dealt with the Prussian Landtag.

Bismarck becomes Minister-President of Prussia
In 1860, the Prussian Minister of War presented to the Landtag (the Prussian Parliament) a plan that would restructure the Prussian army and increase its size. However, the liberals in the Landtag objected to this plan, mainly because taxes would have to be raised to pay for the reforms. The Prussian King, Wilhelm I, was furious as he believed that the Landtag had no right to block the wishes of his Minister of War. The impasse (deadlock) made the King threaten to abdicate, but, in September 1862, he appointed Bismarck Minister-President. Bismarck was a supporter of the King and he advised Wilhelm to ignore the Landtag altogether and to simply order the Prussian people to pay the taxes. The army reforms went ahead but, in 1864, Bismarck responded to increasing opposition to his policies by disbanding the Landtag altogether.

The row with the Landtag, and more importantly Bismarck's solution to it, clearly illustrate Bismarck's own political attitudes. In his autobiography, published many years after the Landtag row, Bismarck wrote, 'It was a question of who ruled Prussia – the King or parliament . . . I would rather perish with the King than forsake your Majesty in the contest with parliamentary government.' Bismarck believed he was defending the traditional authority of the King against new ideas of parliamentary Liberalism.

Other World Events in . . .

1860 In Italy, Sicilian leaders mount an uprising against the Bourbon monarchy. Giuseppe Garibaldi organises an army of 1,000 Red Shirts to support Victor Emmanuel II as king of a united Italy. The following year, the Kingdom of Italy formally comes into existence.

Following the election of Abraham Lincoln as President of the United States of America, North Carolina secedes (withdraws) from the Union.

Charles Dickens publishes *Great Expectations*.

Section summary
In this section you should have learned that:
- there was a row between the King of Prussia and the Prussian parliament over reforms of the Prussian army;
- the row was really a conflict between the authority of parliament and the power of the King;
- the row was resolved by Otto von Bismarck;
- Bismarck revealed his disregard for Liberalism and parliamentary government.

Bismarck – the Great Debate

Syllabus relevance

Intermediate 2:

Bismarck – the debate over his aims in foreign policy.

Higher:

The process of unification in Germany.

At a glance

Prussia was victorious in three wars, against Denmark in 1864, Austria in 1866 and France between 1870 and 1871. The result of these wars was an increase in the power of Prussia and the unification of Germany. Ever since, historians have argued over how important Bismarck was to the process of unification.

How important was Bismarck to unification?

There are three main opinions:

1. Bismarck's importance is that he operated like an architect who had a master plan, which he followed in order to build a unified Germany.

2. Bismarck acted as a catalyst who sped up change which would have happened anyway. According to this argument, changes such as the Zollverein, the spread of railways and growing Nationalism would have eventually united Germany.

> *Catalyst* – something, or someone, which causes, or speeds up, reactions and events.

3. Bismarck had the political skill to take advantage of circumstances as they arose and over which he often had no direct control. Supporters of this view believe Bismarck was an opportunist, taking advantage of situations as they arose.

Did Bismarck have a master plan?

Be careful if you are arguing that Bismarck had a master plan. Students often refer to a conversation that Bismarck was supposed to have had with a British politician, in which he outlined how he intended to unite Germany, as evidence of a master plan. However, there is no proof that the conversation ever took place – an account of the alleged conversation only appeared nearly 20 years after the events happened! It is also difficult to decide if Bismarck himself was always telling the truth, especially in his memoirs.

In 1890, Bismarck wrote 'I was like a man wandering in a forest. I knew roughly where I was going but I didn't know exactly where I would come out of the wood at.' Was Bismarck just being modest?

So what is the correct answer to the question 'Did Bismarck have a master plan?' The safest answer, and the one nearest to the truth, is that Bismarck used his talents to unite Germany, but that he was very aware of circumstances, coincidences and other factors which helped him to achieve his aims. Bismarck has been likened to a card player who played his hand very well, even though he did not deal the cards.

You will return to the debate over Bismarck's plans later but you should remember that historical debate must be based on hard evidence and facts. Bismarck fought three wars that resulted in unification. What are the facts about those wars?

As you work through the next section, be aware of the debate and be ready to answer questions that ask you to explain why unification happened rather than to tell the straight narrative.

Section summary

In this section you should have learned that:

- historians still argue over the importance of Bismarck to the story of German unification;
- some say he was the main reason why Germany was united;
- some argue that unification was the inevitable result of economic and political trends in Europe;
- other historians say that unification was mainly the result of lucky opportunism.

The Wars of Unification

Syllabus relevance
Intermediate 2:
> The wars of unification: Bismarck's methods of isolating his opponents and manipulating opportunities; the war with Denmark and its results; the dispute with Austria over the treatment of Holstein; the war of 1866; Bismarck's negotiations with Napoleon III; the Spanish Candidature; the Franco-Prussian war and the Proclamation of the German Empire.

Higher:
> Reasons for the emergence of Germany as a nation state; the process of unification in Germany.

Bismarck's method of unification relied on an efficient army, as can be seen from a speech that he gave to the Landtag after his appointment as Minister-President, in which he argued that unification could not be achieved:

> 'by speeches and majority votes – that was the mistake of 1848 and 1849. Germany does not look to Prussian Liberalism, but to its power . . . Not by speeches and majority verdicts will the great decisions of the time be made . . . but by iron and blood.'

The first war of unification – Denmark
Bismarck's first step in weakening Austria's power was a war with Denmark.

In 1863, Christian IX became King of Denmark. Christian wanted more power over the two areas on the Danish-German Confederation border called Schleswig and Holstein. Consequently, the Danish parliament passed a constitution which incorporated Schleswig into a new Danish kingdom, using the justification that most of the population of Schleswig was Danish.

Bismarck argued that the action was a threat to the European monarchies and suggested that a combined Prussian and Austrian force should attack Denmark. With Britain and France remaining neutral, Denmark was quickly defeated and Prussia gained the glory as defender of German interests. At the Treaty of Vienna, which marked the end of the war, Denmark gave up its claims to Schleswig and Holstein. However, no agreement was reached about what was to happen to the two border states until August 1865 when, at the Convention of Gastein, it was agreed that Holstein would be governed by Austria and Schleswig by Prussia.

What did Bismarck gain from the conflict with Denmark?
- Prussia's status within the German Confederation was boosted since it looked as if Prussia was a supporter of German Nationalism against the threat of Denmark.
- The recently reformed Prussian army was tested in an 'easy' war before any conflict with Austria erupted.
- Bismarck knew that if Prussia was to be the most powerful state in Germany, Austrian power would have to be weakened – but not yet. At the Convention of Gastein, Austria was politically and militarily cornered by Bismarck as Austria could not refuse to get involved in the row with Denmark if it wanted to keep its influence over the German Confederation. A war with Austria could therefore be provoked when it suited him.

The second war of unification – Austria
Prussia v Austria, 1866
In the 'Great Debate' about Bismarck's role in the unification of Germany, some historians support the view that Bismarck was an opportunist who used coincidental events to his advantage – in other words that events simply played into Bismarck's hands. Yet it is clear that Bismarck deliberately planned the conflict with Austria.

How did Bismarck put his plans into action?
It is vital in any consideration of Bismarck's importance to unification to understand what he did to prepare for military victory. The most pressing issue that Bismarck had to deal with was the possibility that in any war, the other European powers might decide to support Austria or try to grab influence for themselves. The two main powers Bismarck had first to 'neutralise' were Russia and France.

Making friends with Russia

Bismarck wanted to ensure that when Prussia fought Austria, Russia would not get involved.

Although recent historians have said that what happened next was not part of Bismarck's deliberate plan to isolate Austria, you can still use it as part of your argument.

In 1863, a nationalist revolt broke out in present day Poland (which was then a part of Russia). The Polish aim was to break away from Russia and create their own country. Although most of Europe was sympathetic to the Poles, Bismarck gained Russian friendship by stopping Polish refugees escaping into Prussia. By 1865, Bismarck was fairly certain that Russia, formerly a friend of Austria, was now less likely to take sides against Prussia in any future conflict between the two countries.

Keeping France neutral

Bismarck knew there was a possibility that France might help Austria since both were Catholic countries and suspicious of Prussia. Bismarck had to make sure that France would not get involved in a war between Austria and Prussia.

In October 1865, Bismarck arranged a meeting with the French leader, Napoleon III, at the French seaside resort of Biarritz. Without making any promises, Bismarck hinted very strongly that France would get extra territory, possibly in the Rhineland, if France stayed out of a war between Prussia and Austria. Napoleon even secretly believed that a war between Prussia and Austria would benefit France.

> **Other World Events in . . .**
>
> **1865** The American Civil War ends. Since it began in 1861, approximately 600,000 Americans have died on both sides – more than in any other conflict in US history. However, slavery has now been abolished in the United States. Less than a week after the war's conclusion, President Abraham Lincoln is assassinated.
>
> In America, the Ku Klux Klan is established in the South to terrorize blacks and maintain white political control over the region.
>
> Lewis Carroll publishes *Alice's Adventures in Wonderland*.

Doing a deal with Italy

Bismarck also knew that Austria was having trouble in Italy. In the 1860s, Austria controlled most of northern Italy. However, Bismarck knew that Austria would have to split its armies if he could persuade Italian nationalists to attack from the south whilst Prussia attacked from the north.

Bismarck suggested a secret alliance between Prussia and Italy. He promised Italy the land around the city of Venice called Venetia if Italy helped Prussia fight a war against Austria. Italy agreed.

By 1866 Bismarck had set the diplomatic scene. He was ready to fight.

War with Austria

Bismarck used the unresolved situation left after the Convention of Gastein in Schleswig-Holstein to complain that Austria was not running Holstein properly and that Austria was stirring up anti-Prussian feelings in Schleswig. Prussian troops marched into Holstein.

Austria asked the German Confederation for support and when some agreed to resist Prussia, Bismarck had what he wanted – an excuse to attack, defeat and take over the smaller German states that supported Austria.

Meanwhile, as part of the agreement between Italy and Prussia, Italy attacked Austria. Austria mobilised all its troops and Bismarck used that as an excuse to claim that Austria was getting ready to attack Prussia. Prussia attacked Austria in July 1866.

On July 3, 1866 a battle was fought at Königgratz. (The battle is also called the battle of Sadowa.) The Austrian army suffered a huge defeat with over 40,000 dead, wounded or taken prisoner compared to the Prussian figures of less than 10,000. Although Austria was now open to Prussian invasion, Bismarck immediately started to look for a way of ending the war.

The Treaty of Prague

The Treaty of Prague ended the war between Prussia and Austria and is a good demonstration of *realpolitik*. Since Bismarck did not want a bitter, resentful Austria, the Treaty of Prague was very lenient.

> *Realpolitik* – a term meaning practical, rather than ideological, political outcomes.

The old German Confederation was abolished and, by the end of 1866, a North German Confederation had been created. Most of it was Prussian territory. There was also a much weaker South German Confederation.

Although some Prussians wanted to punish Austria, the Treaty of Prague was reasonably fair. Austria had to give Venetia to France (who then handed it to Italy) and promise not to become involved in German affairs again. By this, Bismarck achieved his aims.

A key theme in this course is the struggle for power between Prussia and Austria. It had never been Bismarck's intention to destroy Austria, only Austria's influence over Germany. Bismarck did what was necessary to achieve this aim and nothing more. At the same time, Austria now recognised the need for reform within its Empire and the Dual Monarchy of Austria-Hungary was created out of the old Austrian Empire.

A *Kleindeutschland* had been created and it seemed as if Germany was close to unity. Prussian Liberals were so pleased that most of Germany was united that they forgave Bismarck for the earlier row over army reforms. After all, Bismarck had given them unity by 'iron and blood'.

The third war of unification – France

Bismarck and the Franco-Prussian War (1870–1871)
In 1866, the southern states of Germany were still outside the North German Confederation. They only became part of a united Germany after Bismarck's third war – against France in 1870–71.

The war with France is used by historians as an example of Bismarck taking a situation that was outwith his control and using it to his advantage. The facts certainly support such an opinion.

Bismarck could not simply declare war on France. He needed to set up a situation which would make France appear to be in the wrong. Bismarck's chance came when a row broke out over who was to be the next king of Spain.

The Hohenzollern Candidature
In 1868, a revolution in Spain led to a search for a new ruler. A distant relative of the Spanish royal family, called Leopold of Hohenzollern, was found. However, Leopold was a Prussian. France was worried since, in a future conflict, she might be trapped between a strong Prussia to the north of France and a Prussian 'puppet' government in Spain to the south. The French protested strongly and even insisted that the Hohenzollern family should give up their claim to the Spanish throne forever.

The Ems telegram
King Wilhelm of Prussia was on holiday at a health resort called Ems when he got the French demand. Wilhelm politely refused and sent a telegram to Bismarck telling him what had happened and how he intended to reply to the French.

Bismarck saw his chance and altered the telegram slightly so that it appeared the King had insulted the French ambassador by refusing to meet him. Bismarck then sent his version of the Ems Telegram to the French and German newspapers for publication. The edited version of the telegram had the effect that Bismarck intended. The French government responded to the anger of the public over the 'Prussian insult' by declaring war. Bismarck had what he wanted.

Germany unified – at last!
Within a few weeks of France declaring war, the French army was crushed at the battle of Sedan and France surrendered in January 1871. The North German Confederation and the South German States realised their only chance of security was as part of a strong unified Germany. In the Palace of Versailles, just outside Paris, the German princes proclaimed King Wilhelm of Prussia as Kaiser (Emperor) of a unified Germany.

Prussianisation or unification?

Was Germany unified – or Prussianised? There is a view that the process of German unification should really be seen as the story of Prussia's growing power.

Historians still debate the word 'unified'. The word suggests states coming together through choice, but Bavaria was bribed by Bismarck to join the new Germany and many smaller states still believed they had been defeated and absorbed by Prussia rather than choosing to unify.

> ### The German Flag
> Since 1848, the German flag had been the black-red-yellow tricolour which is in use today. However, when the German Empire was created in 1871, Bismarck chose a black-white-red flag which reinforced north German traditions and Prussian dominance. The Prussian flag was black and white, whilst red was a predominant colour used in the flags of the north German states joining the new Empire. This flag was gradually abandoned after World War I and abolished in 1921.

Furthermore, the Prussian King became the German Kaiser and Bismarck became the German Chancellor whilst Prussian taxes and laws became German taxes and laws. Such evidence suggests that the German states had been 'Prussianised' rather than unified. Whatever the arguments, however, the fact remains that an independent German Empire existed from 1871.

Section summary

In this rather long section you should have learned that:

- Prussia fought and won three wars between 1864 and 1871;
- the three wars were all very important in the story of unification;
- the wars were against Denmark, Austria and France;
- Bismarck used diplomacy and planning to make sure that Prussia won;
- Bismarck manipulated developing situations to Prussia's advantage;
- by 1871 Germany was unified, but it was a Germany under the influence of a very strong Prussian state.

Practise your skills

'There was nothing inevitable about German Unification. Although Bismarck made good use of his opportunities, he would not have succeeded without good luck.' Do you agree?

This question's **topic** is mainly about Bismarck's role in the process of German unification.

The first part of the question refers to the argument that unification would have happened anyway, regardless of Bismarck, because of the pressures that were increasing in the 19th century. The second part of the question asks about Bismarck's importance. Your **task** is to decide how far Bismarck's skills were important, how far he was favoured by opportunity and also what other factors were pushing Germany towards unification.

In your **introduction,** start by indicating the three sections of this essay – firstly sketch the developments which laid the foundations of unification before the 1860s such as Prussian economic power, the Zollverein and Austria's declining power. Secondly, outline the importance of Bismarck's diplomacy. Finally, raise the issue of circumstances which Bismarck used to his advantage. In other words, signpost the main directions your essay will take.

It is vital in the main body of your **essay** to demonstrate your knowledge of this topic. Do not waffle – be precise and accurate:

- Explain more fully why Prussia was seen as a focus for nationalist hopes before 1860. How realistic is the case that German unification was inevitable?
- The bulk of your answer must be on Bismarck – his diplomacy and strategy, his three wars and how he 'Prussianised' the German states.
- Within your section on Bismarck, it is inevitable that you will deal with situations and events which were outwith Bismarck's control but which he used to his advantage. Consider their importance: would Bismarck have been so successful without these events? Or does the importance of these events lie in the way Bismarck used them for his own ends? Was Bismarck a catalyst for change?

The questions raised in this section are vital to your overall answer. Look back at the title and you will see all of these questions are part of it.

In your **conclusion,** you must sum up your main points and decide how far Bismarck was responsible for German unification:

- Certainly, without a reformed army, a revived economy, nationalist enthusiasm and several coincidental pieces of good fortune such as the Hohenzollern Candidature, Bismarck could not have united Germany.
- But it is certainly not wise to argue that Bismarck was just lucky in the sense that he was the 'right man in the right place at the right time'. A suitable conclusion could be to argue that Bismarck was a catalyst and, although he did not control them, he had the ability to use the opportunities events presented.

Honesty check

If you didn't include these points do you now understand them? If not, use these gaps in your knowledge as points to revise or to ask your teacher/tutor about.

The German Empire, 1871–1914: A Unified State

Syllabus relevance

Intermediate 2:
   This section is not part of the Intermediate 2 history course.
Higher:
   A study of the political character of the new nation state in Germany, 1871–1914, with particular reference to the exercise of its authority and the impact of Nationalism on the international relations of the new state.

Germany's Foreign Policy, 1871–1914

At a glance
Between 1871 and 1914, the foreign policy of the German nation state was controlled by two people – Bismarck until 1890 and then Kaiser Wilhelm II.

After 1871, Bismarck wanted to protect the new nation of Germany. To do this, he created a complex web of alliances. Some historians refer to this as the 'Bismarck system'. Others call it 'a balance of tensions'.

When Kaiser Wilhelm II took over the direction of German foreign policy in 1890, he wanted to increase German influence in the world. His foreign policy antagonised and scared other countries so that, by 1914, the Kaiser faced powerful enemies and Europe was divided into 'two armed camps'.

If a question comes up in the exam about German foreign policy it will almost certainly be about the years between 1871 and 1914. In other words, you must include information about Bismarck's foreign policy after 1871 AND the policy of the Kaiser between 1890 and 1914.

Other World Events in . . .

1871 Following its defeat in the Franco-Prussian War, France cedes (gives up) Alsace and part of Lorraine to Germany and allows an army to occupy the country until a war indemnity (compensation) of five billion francs is paid.

The Pope's power to rule territory in Italy is reduced to the Vatican City.

Lewis Carroll publishes a follow up to *Alice's Adventures in Wonderland* called *Through the Looking Glass*.

Journalist Henry Stanley finds the missing Scottish explorer David Livingstone on the edge of Lake Tanganyika in Central Africa.

Sixteen-year-old Euphemia Allen composes *Chopsticks*, a single finger piano tune.

Remember, questions about foreign policy after 1871 have nothing to do with unification before 1871. Be careful not to include irrelevant information.

Bismarck's Foreign Policy, 1871–1890

Bismarck's foreign policy was designed with one purpose in mind – to protect the newly unified Germany. To do this, Bismarck had three aims.

Aim 1 – Keep France isolated

Bismarck believed that the main threat to future German security came from France's desire for revenge. He also believed that if France could make alliances, Germany would face danger. Bismarck therefore made alliances with the two other European land powers, Austria-Hungary and Russia, in order to prevent France gaining them as allies.

You should know about:

- The Three Emperors' League (*Dreikaiserbund*) which was set up in 1873 between Germany, Austria-Hungary and Russia. It was only a loose friendship between the three powers, but nevertheless excluded France. The *Dreikaiserbund* was made more formal in 1881 when the three members agreed to remain neutral if one of them was attacked by another power.
- The Dual Alliance (1879) between Austria-Hungary and Germany promised that if either country was attacked by Russia, the other would come to their aid. This treaty remained secret.
- The Triple Alliance (1882) was signed by Germany, Austria-Hungary and Italy and agreed that if one of the countries was attacked by France, the other two would remain neutral.
- The Reinsurance Treaty (1887), signed by Germany and Russia. It promised that if one country was at war, the other would remain neutral unless Russia attacked Austria-Hungary or Germany attacked France. This Treaty was to be renewed every three years.

Remember that Bismarck's alliances were not intended to be used aggressively. His priority was to protect his 'creation', Germany.

Aim 2 – Make friends with Austria-Hungary and Russia

This was difficult because Russia and Austria-Hungary were rivals, especially in the Balkans. Bismarck believed that any dispute there could lead to war between Austria-Hungary and Russia, a view that was proved correct in 1914! Such a war would upset Bismarck's system of alliances and force Germany to take sides. Bismarck's main aim therefore was to prevent conflict between Austria-Hungary and Russia and to avoid offending either power. This explains why Bismarck tried to keep his Dual Alliance with Austria-Hungary secret from the Russians and also to keep the *Dreikaiserbund* alive. It also partly explains why Bismarck was keen to bring peace to the Balkans at the Congress of Berlin.

Aim 3 – Win international respectability

Bismarck had fought and won three wars in seven years so now had to convince other powers that Germany was a satisfied and peaceful nation which posed no further threat to the peace of Europe.

In 1877, Russia had grabbed land in the Balkans after a war with Turkey, but the rest of Europe, especially Austria-Hungary, was worried about Russian ambitions in the Balkans. Bismarck used the situation to his advantage and appeared to soothe international tensions by helping to avoid a major war breaking out in the region. Described as the 'honest broker', Bismarck was seen at the Congress of Berlin to be a peace maker in Europe and a respected statesman.

> *Broker* – a person who does deals and facilitates the reaching of agreements between possible enemies.

When you are asked to assess the success of Bismarck's foreign policy, the best answer is to argue that in the short term it looked successful. In the long term it is easy to argue that the actions taken by Bismarck eventually led to the First World War – but that ignores the actions of the Kaiser and how he worsened an already difficult situation.

By 1890, Germany seemed to be secure and strong, but can Bismarck be blamed for leaving the new Kaiser with a very tense and suspicious Europe?

Section summary

In this section you should have learned that:

- Bismarck created a web of alliances in Europe which left France isolated;
- Bismarck tried to gain international respectability;
- Bismarck found it difficult to keep Austria-Hungary and Russia as allies.

The Kaiser's Foreign Policy, 1890–1914

A standard interpretation of the Kaiser's running of German Foreign Policy after 1890 is to compare it unfavourably with Bismarck's policies. Traditionalist historians argue that the Kaiser was incompetent, unable to keep Bismarck's fine balancing of alliances operating and took Germany into the disasters of World War One because of his own weaknesses and poor judgement.

On the other hand, revisionist historians claim that it was the 'Bismarck system' which created a balance of tension in Europe and led eventually to the Great War. Do not forget that the Kaiser inherited problems from 'the Bismarck System', a point neatly summed up by the following analogy:

> 'The chickens did not come home to roost until the Kaiser was in charge, but it was Bismarck who hatched the eggs'.

> ### Traditionalists v Revisionists
> Traditionalists are those historians who offer the original interpretation of an historical event, and those who subscribe to it. Revisionists are historians who look back at these events and reconsider the evidence to rewrite – or 'revise' – them. Post-revisionists look at both interpretations to produce a version that contains elements of both traditionalist and revisionist arguments!

The main features to include in an answer about the Kaiser's foreign policy are:

Relations with Russia and France

By 1892, the Kaiser had abandoned a key point in Bismarck's policy – the isolation of France. When Germany did not renew the Reinsurance Treaty with Russia, Russia was annoyed and decided to make an alliance with France. The Franco-Russian alliance of 1894 created a problem for Germany. In a future war, Germany would have to face an enemy on its eastern and western borders. As a result of this threat, the chief of the German army, Count Alfred Von Schlieffen, created a plan that was meant to provide a solution to the problem of a war on two fronts.

Weltpolitik

Weltpolitik (world policy) is best described as the Kaiser's desire to have world influence, not necessarily world domination. The Kaiser, and his advisors, believed that Weltpolitik would encourage patriotism and reduce public discontent with the Kaiser's policies inside Germany. Weltpolitik also pleased businessmen who wanted colonies to trade with, industrialists who wanted a large navy since shipbuilding meant large orders for coal and steel, and German naval officers who wanted a larger navy to gain prestige in the world.

'A place in the sun'

Many people think this famous phrase, said by Chancellor Bülow, means Germany wanted colonies in sunny areas such as Africa and the Far East. It doesn't. The 'place in the sun' meant Germany wanted equality of treatment and equal status with the other Great Powers. Certainly Germany did want more colonies but that was because all important nations had colonies. Why shouldn't Germany have its status symbols?

Was Germany under Kaiser Wilhelm II responsible for World War I?

You are unlikely to get this sort of question because a full answer would require you to look at the actions of other countries. However, you should be aware of what the Kaiser did to increase the tension in Europe before 1914. For example:

- the naval race with Britain;
- the Moroccan crises, which not only angered France but made the rest of Europe see the Kaiser as an unpredictable and possibly dangerous neighbour;
- the Kaiser's support for Austria-Hungary in the Balkans. Eventually, Germany's 'blank cheque' promise of help to Austria-Hungary in its dispute with Serbia and Russia after the Sarajevo assassination led directly to the First World War.

In conclusion, Bismarck's nightmare became reality. Not only had France found an ally in Russia but the Ententes (or friendly agreements) that Britain made with France and Russia meant that Germany was now faced with powerful enemies on land and sea. Germany was surrounded politically and militarily.

In 1914, the Kaiser allowed Germany to get dragged into a Balkan war, which Bismarck had always tried to avoid. The crisis in the Balkans triggered an explosion that had its roots in Bismarck's 'balance of tensions' but was made more volatile by the Kaiser's actions.

> ### Section summary
> In this section you should have learned:
> - that the Kaiser is often blamed for allowing Germany to drift into war;
> - that some historians argue the Kaiser inherited problems from Bismarck which he was unable to resolve;
> - what is meant by Weltpolitik;
> - how the Kaiser pursued his policy of Weltpolitik;
> - how the Kaiser's actions increased international tensions.

Practise your skills

'Nationalism was the driving force of German Foreign Policy under Kaiser Wilhelm II in a way it had not been under Bismarck after 1871.' Do you agree with this statement?

This is a 'theme' question with the emphasis on Nationalism. You should also check what you are meant to do. Your answer must be about the period between 1871 and 1914 only and should not be the story of unification.

You must compare the foreign policies of Bismarck and the Kaiser. Focus on the motives behind their policies and especially consider how important Nationalism was.

Start by outlining why Nationalism was important to both policy makers, but that they had different interpretations of the meaning and uses of Nationalism. To Bismarck, Nationalism meant the protection of the newly united Germany. In contrast, the Kaiser saw Nationalism as expansionist and as a means of extending German influence around the world, which ultimately increased tension within Europe and suspicion of Germany's ambitions.

Begin the main body of your essay by drawing distinctions between the ways that Nationalism 'drove' Germany, but remember to demonstrate your knowledge by supporting your claims with evidence:
- Emphasise the contrast between Bismarck and the Kaiser. The easy way to do this is to look at Bismarck's aims – protection of Germany by isolating France, keeping Britain neutral, balancing Austria-Hungary and Russia as friends of Germany, but avoiding involvement in the Balkans.
- In contrast, the Kaiser's policies alienated Russia and Britain, provided France with allies and, by encouraging Austro-Hungarian ambition in the Balkans, the Kaiser took Germany to a point in 1914 that was to lead to disaster in World War I.
- This means you must deal with key points such as the alliance systems, Bismarck and the Kaiser's relations with other countries and the motives for their actions.

Finish your essay by summing up the different ways in which Nationalism influenced the foreign policy of Bismarck and the Kaiser. You could also argue that Germany did not take two completely different directions in foreign policy and that in many ways the Kaiser inherited difficulties created by Bismarck. The difference lay in the way Nationalism was used for differing purposes. You could conclude by suggesting that whilst Nationalism had created Germany, it also destroyed Germany.

> ## Honesty check:
> If you did not include these points do you now understand them? If not, use these gaps in your knowledge as points to revise or to ask your teacher/tutor about.

German domestic policy between 1871 and 1914

Any question about German domestic policy will usually ask about the years between 1871 and 1914, so an answer on this topic must include information about Bismarck as Chancellor between 1871 and 1890 AND also Kaiser Wilhelm II who was in charge of policy between 1890 and 1914.

Remember: domestic policy means developments inside Germany.

To make it easier to study, this unit is broken into two parts. The first part deals with Bismarck as Chancellor from 1871–1890. The second part deals with Kaiser Wilhelm II.

At a glance

After 1871, Bismarck's main concern was protecting the newly unified Germany. He wanted to maintain the influence and power of Prussia and the Kaiser, while at the same time making sure there were no challenges to his authority. So, in summary, there are three key areas you should concentrate on in any answer about Bismarck's work in Germany after 1871:

- the constitution;
- the struggle with the Catholic Church;
- his struggle with Socialism.

Bismarck as Chancellor of Germany, 1871–1890

The Constitution

Bismarck used the new constitution as a way of maintaining Prussian power over Germany.

Germany's constitution, made law in April 1871, appeared to provide a democratic form of government that would guarantee the autonomy of individual states. However, it was really a means of maintaining

> *Autonomy* – the right to self-govern and the power to exercise this right.

Prussian power. The Reichstag (German parliament) was democratically elected, but the ministers in charge of individual departments were chosen by the Kaiser and were in no way accountable to the elected Reichstag or the public. The Bundesrat was an assembly representing the separate German states. Each state sent representatives but they were not elected. As the largest state, Prussia sent the most representatives (17 out of 58). But, since he controlled Prussia, Bismarck controlled the Bundesrat and was also its chairman! Furthermore, since only 14 votes were required to veto (block) important changes, Prussia (ie Bismarck) was able to do so whenever they wished! The Reichstag had very limited power to make new laws: laws could only be passed if both the Reichstag and the Bundesrat approved them.

So, while the constitution seemed democratic and modern, real power was still in the hands of Bismarck and Prussia.

Some historians have argued that, by accepting a new constitution and operating within it, Bismarck cannot be described as authoritarian. However, the point is that the new constitution was used by Bismarck for his own purposes. Bismarck's actions are well illustrated in his dealings with the National Liberals in the Reichstag. Bismarck was not a Liberal, but he knew that under the rules of the Constitution he needed support from a majority of Reichstag representatives if his policies against other groups in Germany, for example the Catholics, were to be successful. The National Liberals had a large majority in the Reichstag. You will not be surprised to learn, therefore, that Bismarck allied himself to that party, at least while it suited him to do so.

The struggle with the Catholic Church

The new nation state was young and potentially unstable. Bismarck knew that within the new Germany there were tensions and that if they were allowed to grow, these tensions could tear Germany apart. Bismarck believed Catholics posed a potential threat to the stability and security of Germany.

In 1870, Pope Pius IX declared the doctrine of papal infallibility. This meant that whenever the Pope decided on a particular policy or practice, it must be accepted and followed by all Roman Catholics. Bismarck was concerned that Catholic Germans might follow the Pope's rulings rather than German national laws and that this would weaken his own authority. Bismarck also disliked Catholic control over many schools, since he believed young Germans should be encouraged to be patriots first and Catholics second.

One third of the German population was Catholic, but they were split between modernists and traditionalists. It was the latter who supported the Doctrine of Papal Infallibility. Bismarck used the split to start the *Kulturkampf*, which literally means 'cultural struggle' but in real terms meant the attempt by Bismarck to break the power of Catholicism in Germany.

The May Laws
The purpose of the May Laws (all anti-Catholic laws passed between 1873 and 1875) was to limit the authority of the Catholic church and reinforce the authority of the state. You should be able to provide specific examples of these laws, for example:
- control over appointment of Bishops;
- new wedding laws.

However, you must always stress that the reason behind the May Laws was Bismarck's belief that state power should be enforced, and therefore be stronger than any 'outside' influence that might weaken the new German state.

Why did Bismarck abandon the *Kulturkampf*?
Remember Bismarck's priority was the unity and strength of Germany. By the late 1870s, it became clear that the *Kulturkampf* was damaging the unity of Germany as more and more people, both Catholic and Protestant, opposed Bismarck's actions. At this time, Bismarck was also more concerned with another 'threat' to Germany – Socialism.

Socialism was growing in Germany in the late 1870s and Bismarck believed it to be a threat to his power and German unity. But before Bismarck could take action against the socialists he had to secure his position in the Reichstag. Remember that Bismarck only linked himself with a political party in the Reichstag as long as it was useful to his aims. By the late 1870s, the National Liberals were losing seats in the Reichstag but support for the Conservatives and the new Socialist Democrat Party (SPD) was growing. Bismarck needed allies.

Without hesitation, Bismarck turned to the new and growing Catholic Centre Party which disliked Socialism! Almost overnight Bismarck abandoned the *Kulturkampf*. Bismarck also adopted policies that made him popular with the Conservatives. Bismarck was now ready to take on the Socialists.

The struggle with Socialism

Socialism was an internationalist ideology with slogans such as 'workers of the world unite.' Internationalism is the opposite of Nationalism and such ideas challenged German identity – Bismarck could not tolerate such a challenge to his authority.

'whips and sugar plums'

Bismarck controlled Germany in a way which some historians refer to as 'the iron fist in the velvet glove.' This means that at times Bismarck used repressive laws to damage opponents but, when it suited him, he relaxed the pressure and offered concessions. Bismarck himself called his policies a combination of 'whips and sugar plums.' This mixture of policies can be seen in Bismarck's dealings with the Socialists.

> ### Socialism
> Socialists believed in fair shares for all and that could mean the wealthy losing some of their riches. Socialists argued that since the working classes created wealth through their labour – for example digging coal – why should they not share more in the profits of the industry. Why should they not get higher wages and work less hours? Socialism was seen as a threat by those who held power and had influence. Land owners, factory owners, politicians – in fact, anyone who lived comfortably considered Socialism to be a threat. Because Socialists wanted to improve the living and working conditions of the 'have nots' in society, the 'haves' tended to see Socialism as a threat to their standard of living.

Bismarck was not foolish enough to believe that ideologies could be destroyed by banning them. Support for the SDP continued to grow, so Bismarck used contrasting tactics.

Against the hard line Socialists, Bismarck used force ('whips'), such as arresting Socialist leaders, expelling them from Germany and closing down Socialist newspapers. On the other hand Bismarck knew he could attract support from the working classes if he took steps to improve living and working conditions – these were the reforms Bismarck referred to as 'sugar plums'. As part of his campaign to counter the influence of Socialism, Bismarck therefore began a programme of 'State Socialism' which was to improve the conditions of German workers. In 1883, for example, medical insurance and sick pay were introduced, whilst 1889 saw the introduction of old-age pensions. The reforms were not as generous as the SPD had promised, but they were enough to please the working classes and tempt many away from their support for Socialism.

The end of Bismarck

By 1890, Bismarck had made many enemies and the new Kaiser, Wilhelm II, who came to the throne in 1888, no longer wanted German policy to be directed by an old man. In 1890 Bismarck was 75. The Kaiser, not yet 30, believed he could run Germany more effectively. A clash of these authority figures was inevitable. Remember the structure of the German Constitution. Only the Kaiser had the power to remove the Chancellor and that is precisely what he decided to do. Bismarck was not prepared to see his power taken away from him, so he resigned in March 1890.

Section summary

In this section you should have learned that:

- Bismarck's priority was to keep Germany safe and united;
- Bismarck created a constitution which looked democratic but really kept power in the hands of old 'authoritarian' Germany;
- Bismarck believed the ideologies of Catholicism and Socialism were threats to Germany;
- Bismarck's actions as Chancellor demonstrate his pragmatic *realpolitik*.

Practise your skills

Discuss the view that Bismarck preserved the Empire he had created by manipulating different political and religious groups within Germany.

This is an essay about events **inside** Germany – and not foreign policy. The content must include Bismarck's dealings with the National Liberals, the Catholics, the Conservatives and finally the Socialists.

In your **introduction** you should outline the main points of your argument:
- Stress that Bismarck's main concern was the unity of Germany and that his policies were all aimed at achieving that target. It is only by seeing the consistency of that aim that you can make sense of Bismarck's changes of policy.
- Perhaps use 'the iron fist in the velvet glove' image to lead into an explanation of his balancing between repressive and conciliatory measures when dealing with the Catholics and Socialists.

The **main body** of your essay should include the reasons for the *Kulturkampf*, the May Laws and the concessions given to the Catholics. When dealing with the Socialists you should provide detail of the repressive measures and the State Socialism measures adopted by Bismarck.

You must always read the wording of a question carefully. This question asks about 'manipulating different political and religious groups' so your answer must develop this theme. You can explain how Bismarck used Liberals against Catholics and Conservatives and Catholics against Socialists. Another example of his methods could be how, in the 1870s, Bismarck supported free trade (no custom tariffs on foreign imports) when he needed the support of the National Liberals. However, when he needed Conservative support he changed to protectionism (the opposite of free trade) in order to 'buy' the support of groups he wanted to use.

In your **conclusion**:
- Focus on the key point in Bismarck's means of control – as long as he had the co-operation of the Reichstag or the Kaiser, he had the power to make things happen. In other words, you should be balanced between the two sides.
- You could say that, when he lost this support in 1890, Bismarck fell from power. He had failed to find a balance between the modern forces of industrialisation and Socialism on one side and a new, strong-minded Kaiser who believed that he could do a better job than Bismarck.

> ## Honesty check:
> If you did not include these points do you now understand them? If not, use these gaps in your knowledge as points to revise or to ask your teacher/tutor about.

The Kaiser's Germany, 1890–1914

> ### At a glance
> After Bismarck's resignation in 1890, the importance of the Chancellor declined as the authority of the Kaiser increased.

In 1890, Germany was a modern, industrial power – but political reform had not accompanied economic developments. The Kaiser viewed the Reichstag, elected by the people of Germany, as 'an apehouse'. The German Constitution had no restraining influence on the Kaiser, who could appoint and dismiss ministers as he wished. The Kaiser upheld and supported traditional authority and a style of government that was anachronistic (out of date for its time). He declared, 'I intend to rule as well as reign.' It seemed unlikely that the Kaiser would agree to demands for greater democracy.

The Kaiser and the Socialists

After Bismarck's resignation, the Kaiser inherited the problem of what to do about the Socialists and in his dealings with the SPD many of the Kaiser's weaknesses became clear. In 1891, the Social Democrats issued the Erfurt Programme and made certain demands:

- the people, through the Reichstag, should control top government jobs;
- political decisions should be made by representatives of the people in the Reichstag;
- the authority and power of the upper classes should be abolished;
- the rich were to pay most tax.

The policies of the Socialists were a direct challenge to the power of the Kaiser and the ruling class.

The Kaiser believed the SPD was preaching revolution – Was this true?

Before 1914, the majority of SPD members were politicians who hoped that they could improve living and working conditions by working through the parliament. There was therefore the chance to compromise with the moderates within the SPD, but the Kaiser did not want compromise. He surrounded himself with so-called 'advisers' from a similar social class to himself who shared his attitudes and only told him what he wanted to hear.

Did the Kaiser have a coherent policy?

When assessing the Kaiser's control over Germany between 1890 and 1914, it is difficult to escape the difficulties caused by the inconsistencies of his policies. The only thing he was consistent about was his desire to hold on to as much power and personal authority as he could.

The Kaiser offended many working class Germans when he made statements that questioned their patriotism. His attempted return to 'iron fist tactics' through anti-Socialist laws angered many of the working class, even though the new laws were being blocked in the Reichstag. Therefore the Kaiser was left with an angry working class which continued to support the SPD. The Kaiser even talked about using the army to attack German workers and how the army could, in certain circumstances, ignore national laws. It looked as if the Kaiser was trying to be an old-fashioned ruler from the early 19th century.

> ### Other World Events in . . .
>
> **1900** In China, the Boxer Rebellion breaks out. Foreign diplomats and missionaries are attacked by Nationalists, who hope to expel foreign influences from China. The United States, Japan and some European nations send military forces to put down the uprising.
>
> Sir Arthur Conan Doyle, the creator of Sherlock Holmes, writes numerous articles and pamphlets in defence of the British development of concentration camps during the Boer War, for which he is knighted.
>
> *The Wonderful Wizard of Oz* by Frank L Baum is published in America.

The Kaiser's actions and statements showed how undemocratic his attitudes were and how unpredictable and unstable he was. Such an image was not good for a modern country already viewed with suspicion by the other Great Powers.

What was the legacy of the Kaiser?

Some historians argue that the Kaiser was prepared to use an aggressive foreign policy in order to distract attention from domestic problems.

It is true that the Kaiser represented old traditional authority and that such attitudes seemed inappropriate in modern Germany. However, it is important not to overplay the idea of opposition to the Kaiser. Until 1918, he was a respected, even loved, leader simply because of who he was. It took the shock of defeat in World War I to increase discontent with the autocratic rule of the Kaiser and provoke a revolution.

Section summary

In this section you should have learned that:

- the Kaiser wanted to rule as well as reign, meaning that he wanted a return to the 'old order' ideas of authoritarian rule;
- the Kaiser disliked democracy, called the Reichstag 'an apehouse' and had almost unlimited power within Germany;
- the policies of the Kaiser were very inconsistent;
- the personality of the Kaiser was very unstable;
- opposition to the monarchy was centred in the SPD, but the Kaiser remained popular within Germany before 1914.

Practise your skills

'The real problem of Germany under Wilhelm II was not his inconsistency, but rapid social change which was making the German constitution unworkable.' Do you agree?

This essay is about Germany under the Kaiser between 1890 and 1914. The three 'topics' within the title are the Kaiser's inconsistency, rapid social and economic change and the constitution.

The question is asking you to decide what the greatest pressure for change within Germany was between 1890 and 1914. Explain and describe the growing discontent with the Kaiser and then weigh that against the economic and social changes that were increasing pressure for constitutional change.

In your **introduction** you must state what you will do.
- Outline the economic and social pressures for change.
- Explain why some people believed the constitution was in need of reform.
- Explain why the Kaiser's actions led to increased discontent within Germany before 1914.

In the **main body** of this essay, you must demonstrate your knowledge of this. Do not waffle – be precise and accurate:
- It would be a good start to explain the growth of Socialism and the increasing urbanisation of Germany which was leading to demands for political reform. When the Kaiser's repressive actions against the Socialists failed, he revealed his inconsistency by offering concessions to the Socialists.
- Show your knowledge of the political system in Germany. By asking if the Constitution was becoming unworkable, the question is really asking what you know about the Constitution, how it should work, what was the power of the Kaiser and if it was appropriate for a modern state.
- Authority rested in the hands of the Kaiser, his Chancellor and the Bundesrat, which reflected the interests of the royal rulers of the individual German states. Their attitudes were hardly reformist and many German industrialists and aristocrats were also unwilling to give up their power and authority.

Remember that at this time the Kaiser was following an aggressive foreign policy, which some historians say served to distract the population from protesting about the government. But do not get involved in foreign policy. This is an essay about pressures inside Germany.

In your **conclusion** you should:
- refer back to the problems highlighted in the original question;
- make a decision based on that question.

The wisest course is to claim that both the Kaiser's actions and social and economic pressures were putting great strain on the constitution. Germany was torn between those who wanted change and those who wanted no change.

> Honesty check:
> If you did not include these points do you now understand them? If not, use these gaps in your knowledge as points to revise or to ask your teacher/tutor about.

The First World War

1914 On June 28, Archduke Francis Ferdinand, the heir to the throne of the Austro-Hungarian Empire, and his wife are assassinated by Gavrilo Princip, a Serbian Nationalist, in Sarajevo. This is the spark which ignites the build-up of tensions in Europe that had been growing since the end of the nineteenth century.

On July 5, Austria-Hungary secures a promise of unconditional support, a 'blank cheque', from Germany in the event of Austro-Hungarian military action.

On July 23, the Serbian government receives a humiliating ultimatum from Austria-Hungary. The Serbs agree to all aspects of the ultimatum, except for a demand that the Habsburgs participate in an enquiry into the assassination.

On July 28, Austria-Hungary declares war on Serbia. The same day, Russia begins a partial mobilisation against Austria-Hungary in support of the Serbs. Germany warns Russia that if she does not stop this mobilisation, Germany will mobilise against Russia, which Germany does on July 31.

On August 1, Germany declares war on Russia. However, all German strategies centre around the Schlieffen Plan (see page 28), which assumes a war against France, Russia's ally. Consequently, Germany also declares war on France on August 3. The following day, the German army invades Belgium and so Britain declares war on Germany.

Between September 5 and September 10, the Battle of the Marne is fought, halting the German advance through France and establishing a front line on the Western front which remains largely unchanged until 1918.

1915 German U-Boats begin a naval blockade of Britain and a policy of sinking every ship in the English Channel without warning.

On April 22, the Germans make the first use of poison gas, attacking the French lines at Ypres.

On April 25, troops from Australia and New Zealand land at Gallipoli, Turkey, in the hope of attacking the Central Powers from the South. The Allies are defeated in one of the most costly battles of the War.

On May 7, the British Ocean Liner *Lusitania* is attacked by a German U-Boat off the coast of Ireland. The *Lusitania* takes only 18 minutes to sink, causing the death of 1,198 passengers. As some of the dead are Americans, the German government issues an apology for the attack, fearing the United States will be provoked into joining the war.

1916 On February 21, the German Army launches a war of attrition against the French town of Verdun in the hope of lowering French morale. 700,000 men are killed.

From July, the Battle of the Somme is fought for 140 days on a front of 20 miles. Despite the death of over 1·4 million soldiers, only insignificant territorial advances are made by the Allies.

On August 27, Italy declares war on Germany. (This is seen as an attempt by Italy to be on the 'winning' side.)

On December 5, David Lloyd George replaces Herbert Asquith as Prime Minister of Britain.

1917 On March 16, Czar Nicholas II of Russia is forced to abdicate.

On April 6, the United States of America declares war on Germany, provoked by the continued sinking of American ships.

On November 6, the Bolshevik Party seizes control of Russia.

1918 On March 3, the new Communist government of Russia signs the Treaty of Brest-Litovsk, ending Russian involvement in the war. Russia gives up large areas of land to the Germans and agrees to pay a large amount of compensation.

On March 21, the Germans launch a major offensive on the Western Front, hoping to win the war before the arrival of American troops.

In July, the Allies begin a counter-offensive against the Germans. Supported by the introduction of the tank, they are able to make large advances and the German army begins to retreat.

On November 9, Kaiser Wilhelm II abdicates and Germany is declared a Republic. Two days later, an armistice is signed, ending the war. An estimated 10 million people have been killed.

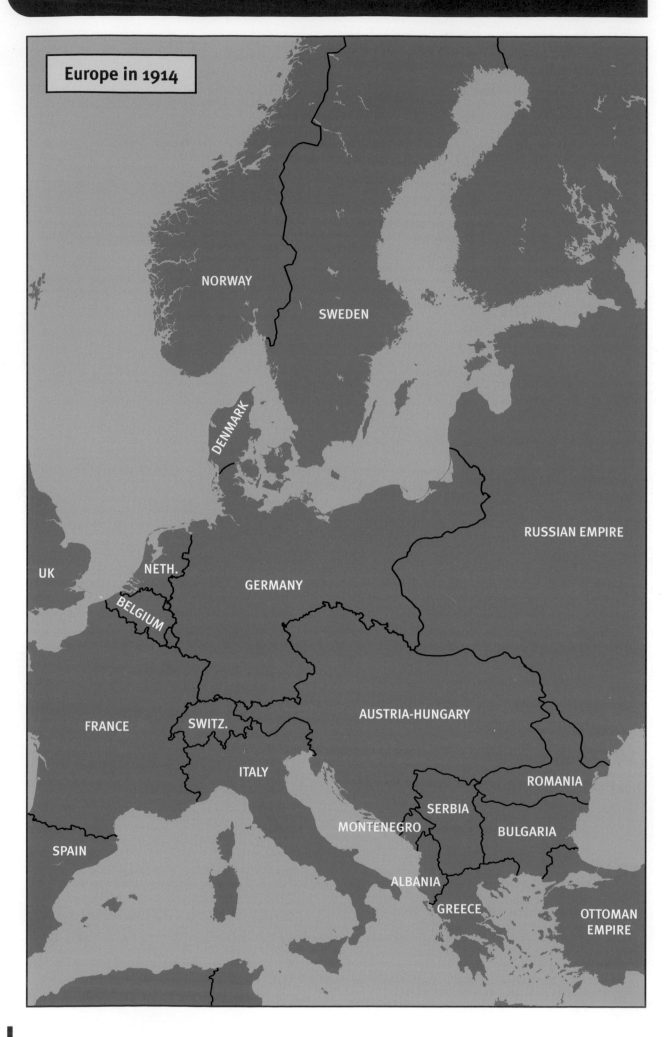

Europe in 1914

Europe in 1919

The Rebirth of German Nationalism, 1918–1939

Syllabus relevance

Intermediate 2:
   This section is not part of the Intermediate 2 History course.
Higher:
   In relation to Germany, the nature of fascism and the reasons for its victory. The nature of fascist authority and the use of power to 1939.

The Weimar Republic and the rise of Hitler, 1919–1933

The new Germany that emerged at the end of the First World War had a new political system called a republic with a new ideology – democracy – based on a written constitution guaranteeing individual freedoms. The new constitution was written in a town called Weimar, hence the 'Weimar Republic'.

The Weimar Republic became identified with failure and defeat and the new political system was challenged by various groups who did not share the political beliefs of this new Germany. One of these groups was the *Nationalsozialistische Deutsche Arbeiterpartei* (National Socialist German Worker's Party) – the Nazis.

Adolf Hitler came to power in 1933 promising the creation of a new Germany with strong leadership in contrast to the lack of direction evident in Weimar Germany. His new ideology was called Nazism.

In this part of the course there are three main questions to prepare for. The first and second questions are closely linked.
1. Why did Weimar Germany fail?
2. How and why did Hitler come to power in Germany?
3. How did Nazism affect the lives of people within Germany between 1933 and 1939?

The chart below summarises the main questions asked about the failure of Weimar and the rest of the work in this unit about the rise of the Nazis looks closely at these ideas.

How far was the Weimar Republic weakened by its own politicians, who conspired against the ideology of the Republic, hoping to further their own 'hidden agendas', and in so doing failed to oppose Hitler's destruction of the system?

How important is the Treaty of Versailles in explaining the problems faced by the Weimar Republic throughout its life?

How important was the survival of 'old Germany' supporters behind the scenes of 'new Germany' in explaining the difficulties faced by the Weimar Republic?

How important do you think these questions are to the rise of Hitler and the fall of the Weimar Republic?

Use this section to make up your mind.

How important were the economic crises of 1923 and 1929 in destroying support for the Weimar Republic?

How far can the Weimar Republic's own constitution be blamed for creating unforeseen problems?

Was Hitler's offer of a strong authority figure that millions could identify with just too strong to resist?

How did the Treaty of Versailles cause problems for the Weimar Republic?

On June 28, 1919, the victorious allies made Germany sign the Treaty of Versailles. Many Germans called the treaty a *Diktat* – a dictated treaty that was forced on them.

The treaty forced Germany to accept blame for causing the war and also for the death and destruction that followed – this was known as the War Guilt Clause. Germany lost all its colonies, much of its industrial resources and some areas of land, whilst its armed forces were severely cut. Germany also had to pay compensation, called reparations, to the victorious powers. This figure was later set at £6,600 million.

Few Germans had expected the treaty to be as harsh as it was. In particular, many Germans refused to accept the War Guilt Clause, arguing that Germany had not been responsible for starting the war. The question of reparations was equally controversial and is seen by many historians as being partially responsible for the economic difficulties Germany faced during the 1920s. However, in comparison with Germany's own treatment of France in 1871 and Russia in 1917, the Treaty of Versailles was relatively mild.

Throughout the 1920s, many Nationalist groups claimed that the new Republic had 'stabbed Germany in the back' by accepting the treaty. These groups identified the Republic with defeat and humiliation. In the economic ruin of the early 1920s, many Germans found it easier to believe the idea that politicians had betrayed Germany in 1919, rather than face the reality that the country could not continue fighting in the last days of the war. In short, they could not accept that, as a result of Weimar politicians signing Versailles, Germany was no longer a world power. The link between defeat and the new democratic government weakened the authority of and respect for Weimar politicians and ultimately led to the collapse of the Republic.

Section summary

In this section you should have learned:
- what the Treaty of Versailles was;
- why Germans were angry about the Treaty of Versailles;
- why the Treaty of Versailles was an important factor in public discontent with the new Republic.

How important was the existence of groups opposed to Weimar's democratic ideology in explaining its difficulties?

Several political groups were opposed to democratic principles. You must be clear why Weimar was opposed by political groups from both the left and right wings of German politics.

Enemies from the Left

In 1919 the Spartacists, who were revolutionary Socialists and who later became known as the Communist Party or KPD, tried to start a revolution to create a new Communist Germany. The Spartacist rising was defeated with great brutality by an alliance between the new SPD government and the regular army. Ten years later, when Hitler was rising to power, the hatred felt by the Communists towards the SPD for destroying the Spartacist rising prevented the left wing from uniting against Hitler in elections.

Opposition from the Right

The new Germany was equally hated by the right wing. When the Weimar government tried to carry out the military cuts imposed by Versailles, German army officers were furious. These officers saw an end to their careers and supported the Kapp *Putsch* (revolution) – an attempt to overthrow the government and bring the Kaiser back.

However, do not think of the right wing as simply a collection of military leaders. The right included many professionals whose early careers had been spent within the Imperial Germany of the Kaiser. Although the government changed after the war and became a democracy, most of the professional classes did not necessarily change their attitudes. All these people still identified with 'old' Germany while working within 'new' Germany. How loyal to the new democracy would these sympathisers of Imperial Germany be when a crisis arose in the early 1930s?

Section summary

In this section you should have learned that:
- between 1918 and 1920 extremists from both the left wing and the right wing of German politics tried to overthrow the new government;
- the new democratic government had many enemies but few friends.

How far can the Weimar Republic's own constitution be blamed for creating unforeseen problems?

The new democratic constitution of Germany was called 'the most perfect democracy on paper' but it had flaws that were exploited by opponents. These flaws were parts of the Constitution intended to make a fair and democratic system but which, ironically, contributed to its collapse. They were:

1. the voting system
2. Article 48 of the Constitution
3. the power of the President.

1. The voting system was based on a form of proportional representation. This should have meant that the election results would closely reflect the wishes of the public. However, in practice it simply meant there was never a clear winner who could provide an essential element in any government – strong leadership. Due to this, a series of coalition governments were set up after deals were made between parties. These coalition governments found it difficult to put into action strong decisive policies. Between 1919 and 1930 there were 13 coalition governments.

   Although the voting system was fair, it was confusing. The system also allowed small, extremist parties such as the Nazis and the Communists to gain some representation in the Reichstag – even if these parties really aimed for the destruction of the new republic.

2. The creators of the Constitution realised that future crises might occur and fast decisive action might be needed to protect the new democracy. Article 48 and the role of the Presidency were created to deal with these problems.

3. Article 48 gave the President (elected every 7 years) the power to rule in an emergency without needing approval from the Reichstag. But what might happen if an extremist politician, such as Hitler, gained control of the Presidency?

Section summary

In this section you should have learned that:

- 'the most perfect democracy on paper' had flaws in it which could be exploited by groups which wanted to destroy the Weimar Republic.

Did the economic crisis of 1923 create long-term problems for Weimar Germany?

The Treaty of Versailles ordered Germany to pay compensation to the victorious allies, but by 1923 France was angry at Germany's repeated failure to pay the instalments on time. Consequently, France invaded the Ruhr, Germany's industrial heartland, aided by Belgium. France intended to use the Ruhr as a source of coal and steel to help rebuild her cities. Any extra steel would then be sold as an additional source of finance. France's clear intention was to take directly the money that she believed was owed by Germany. Instead, German workers went on strike.

The German government printed more and more paper money to pay the strikers, but with no wealth being created the value of the German currency collapsed. By November 1923 German money was worthless. This was a time of hyperinflation. Almost overnight the life savings of millions of Germans became worthless and they blamed the government.

Hyperinflation had a deep impact on the German people, especially the middle classes. It has been described by the historian Louis L Snyder as 'the scar that never healed'.

The German economic crisis of the early 1920s only ended when American money was pumped into the German economy and a time of relative political and economic stability followed.

Section summary

In this section you should have learned that:

- Germany faced a serious economic crisis in 1923, which led to hyperinflation;
- many Germans, hard hit by the hyperinflation, blamed the Weimar Government for their problems.

Gustav Stresemann

Between 1924 and 1929, support for the Nazis slumped at a time when stability returned to the German economy and Germany regained international respectability. It seemed the old enmity between France and Germany was in decline and the mid 1920s have been described as the 'Golden Years' of the Weimar Republic. Much of the success of the Weimar Republic at this time was due to the efforts of one man – Gustav Stresemann.

In August 1923, Stresemann became Chancellor of Germany and brought an end to the passive resistance in the Ruhr. Reparations were once again paid and a new currency, assisted by loans from the USA brought financial stability back to Germany. By 1925, Stresemann was foreign minister and decided on a more subtle strategy in dealing with Germany's neighbours. Rather than seeking conflict, for example by refusing to pay reparations, Stresemann did what he could to meet the demands of the allies. In so doing, Germany gained their trust and, by signing the Locarno Treaty, French fears of Germany were eased a bit. The next year, 1926, Germany joined the League of Nations and it seemed that the old hatreds following the war were fading.

Stresemann's work was important to the German recovery of the mid 1920s, and his death in 1929 from a heart attack left Germany politically weakened during the depression which followed the Wall Street Crash.

1929 – the Turning Point for Germany

In 1928 the Nazis had 12 seats out of 491 in the Reichstag, but by 1930 they had 108 out of 577 (the number of seats in the Reichstag varied from election to election). You can use these figures to introduce an answer about the rise of the Nazis because clearly something must have happened between 1928 and 1930 to increase Nazi support. The answer lies in 1929. In that year, Germany was hit by a double disaster.

The first was the death of Gustav Stresemann. The second disaster was the Wall Street Crash. You do not need to know the economic details of the Crash but you do need to know the results. During the 1920s, American banks had given millions of dollars of loans to Germany, which had helped to create a sense of political stability. However, as they collapsed these banks not only stopped giving these loans but also demanded the immediate repayment of those Germany had already received, sending Germany into depression. Unemployment rocketed and Germany descended into economic chaos. Although hyperinflation did not return, the German public remembered the nightmare of 1923 and 'the scar that never healed'. By 1930 the German public was desperate for a saviour to help them out of the crisis.

Other World Events in . . .

1929

Joseph Stalin expels his rival Leon Trotsky from Soviet Russia, who is later murdered in Mexico.

The Lateran Treaty creates the new sovereign state of Vatican City, ruled by the Pope, and recognises Roman Catholicism as the only state religion of Italy.

Seven rivals of Al Capone's gang are gunned down in Chicago as part of the fight to control the illegal liquor trade (alcohol was banned across America in 1922) in what becomes known as the St Valentine's Day Massacre.

The first Academy Awards ceremony is held in Hollywood.

Ernest Hemingway publishes *A Farewell to Arms*.

The economic crash was the catalyst that transformed the appeal of the Nazis. As the historian AJP Taylor said, 'It was the Great Depression that put the wind in Hitler's sails'.

Section summary

In this section you should have learned that:
- in the mid 1920s, financial support from America made German politics more stable;
- support for extremist parties declined in the mid 1920s;
- the Wall Street Crash of 1929 sparked off a worldwide depression;
- the economic crisis allowed the Nazis to gain support as they said they had the answers to Germany's problems.

Where did the Nazis come from?

In 1930, the Nazis made their big breakthrough into mainstream German politics. The Nazis appeared to be strong and decisive. But where had they come from?

In 1919, the German Workers' Party was just one of many small parties unhappy with the conditions in Germany. In 1921, Adolf Hitler became its leader and changed its name to the National Socialist German Workers' Party. Despite a tiny membership, the Nazis attracted the support of Field Marshall Erich Ludendorff, a noted war hero, and in November 1923 felt confident enough to seize power. Having been promised support from elements of the German army and other conservative groups, Hitler and 3,000 of his followers marched through the streets of Munich. However, the promised support did not emerge and the revolt was crushed by only one hundred policemen. Hitler was arrested and sentenced to five years in prison, although he only served nine months.

The shortness of his sentence is in itself important as it reveals the right-wing sympathies of Weimar politicians, which was a dangerous weakness of the Republic. Remember that when the left-wing Spartacists attempted to overthrow the government in 1919–20 they were murdered, arrested and executed or given long prison sentences. Given his mild punishment, had Hitler found friends in high places of influence?

As a result of the Munich *Putsch*'s failure, Hitler realised that he could not rely on allies outside of his own party to help him wrest power. He also recognised that he would only succeed by working within the existing political system. He is often reported as saying, 'we must hold our noses and enter the Reichstag'. In other words Hitler would campaign for power legally and destroy the system he despised from within.

However, the Nazis were not the only party that despised the ideology and identity of the Weimar Republic. By 1930, Nationalist groups led by Alfred Hugenberg saw the Nazis as a possible route to power. Hitler was happy to use Hugenberg, who owned most of Germany's new cinema industry and hundreds of local newspapers, for his own ends. Hitler saw a way of becoming a nationally known figure very quickly in a pre-televisual age (Hitler had already become the first politician to use a private plane to fly around the country, enabling him to speak in several towns a day during election campaigns). All Hitler needed was the opportunity to spread his message of a new Germany under Nazism. Events in 1929 gave Hitler his opportunity.

Nazi Ideology – What was Nazism?

Most political parties have a clear idea of what they stand for and also a clear plan that is designed to appeal to certain sections of the population.

The Nazis tried to be all things to all people. As one of many small political groups in the early 1920s, the Nazis had to attract attention and support. Hitler outlined his ideas in his book *Mein Kampf* (My Struggle). These included:

The Treaty of Versailles had to be destroyed

The treaty symbolised Germany's humiliation at losing the war and the loss of imperial identity. Most of what happened later can be directly linked to Hitler's aim of destroying the Treaty of Versailles.

Hitler wanted all German-speaking people to live in one enlarged Germany

He said that all Germans had the right to live in Germany. If that meant the country's borders had to be enlarged to occupy lands where Germans lived, then he was prepared to make that happen.

Germans were the master race

Hitler believed Aryans – or Germans – were the master race. Hitler talked about 'inferior' races such as Jews and Slavs as being sub-human – not even real people. The Nazi word for sub-humans was *Untermenschen*. Hitler believed the *Untermenschen* had one purpose in life – to serve the master race.

> ### Aryans
> In *Mein Kampf*, Hitler argued that the German race was superior to all others and was responsible for almost every scientific and artistic advance. However, when he described Germans as being 'Aryan', he was wrong. In fact, Aryans originally came from India and Iran and were far from the blond hair, blue eyed ideal that Hitler believed all Germans should be.

Hitler wanted *Lebensraum* (Living Space)

Hitler claimed that Germany had to have all the land and resources it needed to survive and grow strong, even if it meant taking these things from other countries. This policy aim was called *Lebensraum*. Hitler's foreign policy was expansionist and potentially aggressive. His ultimate target can be seen from this quotation from *Mein Kampf*:

> 'We [must] stop the endless German movement to the south and west, and turn our gaze towards the land in the east . . . If we speak of soil in Europe, we can primarily have in mind only Russia and her vassal [dependent] border states.'

A definition of Nazism could include the following:

- One strong leader. Hitler has been described as 'the buckle holding the belt of Nazism together'.
- Centralised government tried to control everything. Regional and local Nazi organisations were established so that control extended throughout the whole country.
- Only one political party. All opposition was banned.
- Propaganda was used to increase Nazi power and to control the media.
- Racism. Hitler used feelings of Nationalism, patriotism and racism to create an ideology of hatred and a belief that Germans were the master race.
- Anti-Semitism. Hitler claimed that Germany had been stabbed in the back by Jewish politicians in 1918. He blamed Germany's economic problems on Jews. Hitler even claimed Communism was a Jewish plot since the founder of Communism, Karl Marx, was a Jew. By the early 1930s, it suited many Germans to see the Jews as an excuse for Germany's difficulties.

Hitler provided simplistic answers to complex problems. Nazi Germany was an **authoritarian state**, which insisted on obedience to its rules. The following description sums up the aims of a **totalitarian**, authoritarian state – the interest of the State, at the expense of the individual, and opposed to anything outside of the State.

Nazi Germany was a dictatorship, but one which attracted support from people looking for a saviour.

Section summary

In this section you should have learned:

- how the Nazis tried to be all things to all people to attract public support;
- that Nazi ideology was authoritarian and racist;
- that Nazi ideology was a mixture of old and new ideas;
- what is meant by authoritarian.

Can politicians be blamed for Hitler's rise and the collapse of the Weimar Republic?

In January 1933 Hitler was invited to become Chancellor of Germany. In explaining how this came about, you must deal with three main characters – Hindenburg, who was President of the Weimar Republic (do not get confused with Hugenburg, the owner of cinemas and newspapers), von Papen and von Schliecher – who were vital in enabling Hitler's rise to 'legitimate' power.

President Hindenburg was an old war hero who represented old style authority and personified 'Old Germany'. But he was very old, almost senile and the authority of Hindenburg was used by politicians who wanted to undermine Weimar democracy.

President Hindenburg and other Weimar politicians had been acting in an undemocratic way since 1930. For example, Hindenburg, by using Article 48 of the German Constitution, allowed Chancellor Brüning to govern Germany for almost two years without majority support in the Reichstag.

As Hitler and the Nazis rose in popularity – in the July 1932 election, the Nazis won 37% of the vote and 230 out of 608 seats in the Reichstag – Weimar politicians made the mistake of believing that they could use Hitler for their own ends. Hitler was charismatic, and less popular politicians hoped that by allying themselves with him they could ride to power with their Nazi allies. The two politicians most closely associated with this attempt to 'use' Hitler were von Papen and General von Schleicher. Von Papen made the following statement in 1932, memorable for its completely wrong assessment of the situation: 'In six months we'll have pushed Hitler so far into a corner he will be squealing.'

von Papen and von Schleicher

Hitler's rise to power was certainly helped by 'political intrigue'. By the early 1930s, some ambitious Weimar politicians were willing to use the tense times of political extremism and political confusion to their advantage. Two such opportunist politicians were Franz von Papen and Kurt von Schleicher.

Franz von Papen joined the Catholic Centre Party and in 1921 was elected to the Reichstag. However, he had few political allies and it was a surprise when President Hindenburg appointed him Chancellor on 31st May, 1932. By this time, the Nazis were an increasingly popular party and, by lifting the ban on the SA (Hitler's private army), von Papen gained the support of the Nazi Party in the Reichstag.

Von Papen had many political enemies, one of whom was Kurt von Schleicher, who was influential in forcing von Papen to resign in December 1932. Von Papen wanted revenge and began to plot with Hitler in an effort to remove von Schleicher, who had replaced him as German Chancellor.

Von Papen had been developing the support of many right-wing industrial leaders and in early 1933 he used these friendships to pressure Hindenburg into appointing Hitler Chancellor. Von Papen became Vice-Chancellor. He had assured Hindenburg that he would be able to control Hitler. He was wrong. However, he was luckier than von Schleicher (who was murdered during the Night of the Long Knives – see page 48). Von Papen served under the Nazis as German ambassador in Austria and Turkey – not the influential role he had pictured for himself.

As a summary to an answer about Hitler's rise to power, you could say with confidence that without the Great Depression Hitler would have been unable to build up mass support. Nor would he have attracted the attention of right-wing politicians who thought they could use him for their own ends.

In January 1933, Hitler was the Chancellor of a democratic government which he despised and the leader of a coalition government in which the Nazis were a minority. So do not make the mistake of saying that Hitler was 'in power' by January 1933. You must be prepared to explain how Hitler went from legal Chancellor to legal dictator. In other words, what was the Nazi Revolution?

The consequences of the Treaty of Versailles caused both immediate and longer term problems, which undermined public confidence in the new democratic republic. Hitler had a ready-made audience for his promises to destroy the Treaty and restore German honour.

By 1932, politicians such as von Papen and von Schliecher used or supported undemocratic measures in their quest for solutions to Germany's problems. These usually involved securing powerful positions for themselves. Hitler was seen as a 'drummer boy' who could attract attention, and perhaps votes, for whoever could ally with the Nazis. Democratic principles were undermined by those who should have been guarding them.

Those who worked within the system, from civil servants to judges, had grown up during the Kaiser's reign. Old attitudes and preferences did not change just because Germany was now a democracy. A desire for a strong man to lead Germany to safety was a factor in Hitler's rise. After Stresemann's death, the Weimar Republic had no 'strong man' of sufficient appeal.

This diagram summarises the answers to the questions posed in the diagram on page 40 of this book.

Check back to see the original questions.

In 1923, many Germans saw their lives ruined by economic collapse. Recovery based on American loans was artificial and, when the Crash came in 1929, many feared for their futures again. In the economic depression which followed, the Nazis were seen as a defence against an imminent Communist revolution. Their promise of work and bread attracted much support.

The excitement of Nazi propaganda, the offer of easy answers to complex problems and the charismatic appeal of Hitler persuaded many that the Nazi Party could save Germany.

The 'perfect democracy on paper' was confusing to many. The voting system gave toeholds in the Reichstag to undemocratic forces and also resulted in coalition governments unwilling or unable to respond to crises. Public confidence was undermined. Article 48, intended to save Germany in times of crisis, was used to undermine democracy.

Section summary

In this section you should have learned that:
- by 1932 some Weimar politicians were undermining the democratic system from within;
- by 1932 some Weimar politicians hoped to use Hitler to achieve their own anti-democratic ambitions;
- in January 1933 Hitler became Chancellor of Germany legally, within the Weimar Republic's Constitution.

The creation of the Nazi Dictatorship

You should be able to explain clearly the methods taken by Hitler between January 1933 and August 1934 to move from being legal Chancellor in a democratic government to dictator of a totalitarian state. Historians often call this change the 'Legal Revolution'.

You should structure your explanation of the Legal Revolution by dealing with:
- the destruction of democratic government;
- the destruction of opposition to the Party;
- the creation of a totalitarian dictatorship.

The destruction of democratic government

When the Nazis said they would hold their noses and enter the Reichstag, they added that 'sooner or later we will have power.' Hitler knew that the power of the Reichstag would have to be destroyed.

The Reichstag fire

A week before another General Election in February 1933, the Reichstag building caught fire. There is still debate about who started the fire, but Hitler immediately blamed the Communists – they were the most active opposition against Hitler and he argued that they had shown their anti-democratic ideas by burning the Reichstag. Hitler was then able to argue that Germany was under threat of a Communist Revolution and that Article 48 (see page 42) needed to be used. The decree issued by Hitler (under the authority of the President) was called 'A Decree for the Protection of People and State.' However, by banning many freedoms and allowing imprisonment without trial, Hitler was already destroying democracy.

> **Other World Events in . . .**
>
> **1933** The Oxford University Debating Society endorses, by 275 votes to 153, a motion stating 'that this House will in no circumstances fight for its King and Country.'
>
> As a result of the rising anti-Semitism and anti-intellectualism in Germany, Albert Einstein emmigrates to the United States.
>
> The board game Monopoly is invented.
>
> Mohandas K Gandhi begins a hunger strike to protest against British oppression in India.
>
> The first photograph claiming to be of the Loch Ness Monster is taken.

The Legal Dictatorship

Following the election at the beginning of March 1933, the Nazis still only had 43.9% of the popular vote (288 out of 647 seats in the Reichstag). They could only claim a majority by forming a coalition with the Nationalist Party. (Note that this was a very different party to the Nazis.) On March 23, however, the Reichstag passed the Enabling Act, which allowed the Chancellor (i.e. Hitler) to issue laws that the Reichstag could not change – even the signature of the President was no longer required. Non-Nazi members of the Reichstag had been persuaded to vote for the Act through a combination of a false promise that it would only be a temporary measure, which would not be used once the crisis in Germany was over, and intimidation from members of the SA. The Enabling Act effectively killed Weimar democracy and allowed the Nazis to establish a legal dictatorship.

Centralising power

An authoritarian state can tolerate no challenge to its power. Very quickly Hitler made sure that all German states (for example, Bavaria, Bremen and Hamburg) were ruled directly from Berlin and that the individual states had no political voice of their own.

The destruction of opposition to the Party

On July 14 1933, the Nazi government declared the Nazi Party to be the only legal political party in Germany. Without political choice there was no democracy. The Nazis also banned trade unions because Hitler thought the unions might be centres of left-wing opposition.

> ### Section summary
> In this section you should have learned that:
> - Hitler had little real power in January 1933;
> - Hitler used the Reichstag fire and the Enabling Act to create a dictatorship;
> - Weimar democracy was effectively dead by July 14, 1933.

The creation of a totalitarian dictatorship

Hitler still did not feel secure. Behind the scenes, he needed the support of important groups of people – especially the army.

Hitler had already tried to link these powerful groups to the Nazis. In 1931, an alliance of right-wing politicians, Junkers (Prussian noblemen and land owners), senior army officers and the Nationalist ex-servicemen's association was formed and became known as the Hartzburg Front. This organisation helped Hitler with vital financial backing. However, by 1934, the Nazi's private army, the SA, seemed to threaten Hitler's relationship with the army officers.

'The Night of the Long Knives'

The SA had caused much of the violence that disturbed Germany throughout the late 1920s and by 1934 Hitler saw them as at best politically embarrassing and at worst a threat to his security. The leader of the SA was Ernst Röhm. He planned to merge the regular army with the poorly trained SA to make a people's army. The regular army was horrified. This concerned Hitler, as he knew that he still needed the support of the army, especially as he was now planning to combine the offices of Chancellor and President. Hitler knew he had to choose between his old friends in the SA and the regular army officer class. Hitler's elimination of the SA leadership happened on June 30, 1934 – 'The Night of the Long Knives'. Hitler's private bodyguard, the SS, was used to kill many of Hitler's enemies, including Röhm. By ruthlessly murdering suspected enemies, Hitler became more politically secure, whilst the eradication of the SA pleased the regular army.

The Oath of Loyalty and the Death of Hindenburg

In August 1934, President Hindenburg died. The President had been the head of state and the guardian of the Constitution in Weimar Germany, but when Hindenburg died Hitler fused the powers of President and Chancellor to create the dictatorial role of Führer. Earlier, Hitler had arranged for every individual member of the armed forces to take an oath of loyalty to himself. The result was that, by August 1934, Hitler had total power.

Section summary

In this section you should have learned that:

- Hitler was aware that he needed to keep influential right-wing groups in Germany happy;
- the Night of the Long Knives pleased the army;
- the oath of loyalty taken by the army was significant in the consolidation of Hitler's power;
- Hindenburg's death in August 1934 signalled the end of the Weimar Constitution.

Practise your skills

Account for Hitler's rise to power.

This essay is about how Hitler became dictator of Germany.

As part of your answer to this question, you must define 'power'. The words 'account for' mean you have to explain how Hitler achieved such power.

You should indicate in your **introduction** that you know that while Hitler became Chancellor in 1933, real power was not achieved until 1934 – after the Enabling Act, the Night of the Long Knives, the death of Hindenburg, the oath of loyalty and the establishment of Hitler as Führer. These events should only be touched on and explained more fully in the main body of your essay.

By laying out your intentions in the introduction you have made clear you understand the question and also the timescale you intend to cover.

In essence, the outline of this essay is provided for you in the chart on page 40 of this section. You will find yourself referring to developments long before Hitler rose to power, since discontent with the Weimar Republic is an important factor. But beware – the bulk of this essay should focus on the years between 1930 and 1934 and the events mentioned in your introduction, so do not spend too long explaining background detail.

You must deal fully with 'the legal revolution' – how Hitler moved from being Chancellor of a coalition government in January 1933 to Führer by August 1934.

Remember to start each paragraph with a key sentence that outlines the point you will be developing.

In your **conclusion** you should:
- Sum up the reasons why Hitler rose to power, but try to prioritise by deciding which were the most important.
- You might want to finish with a quote. For example, AJP Taylor's observation that 'the Great Depression put the wind in Hitler's sails' is a great quotation to cite. However, you would have to make the point that the depression merely granted him opportunity, it did not sweep him into power. There were many other factors.

> Honesty check:
> If you did not include these points do you now understand them? If not, use these gaps in your knowledge as points to revise or to ask your teacher/tutor about.

Life in Nazi Germany, 1933–39

The German Economy

When Hitler became Chancellor in 1933, the German economy was close to collapsing: unemployment stood at 25·9% and the standard of living in Germany was extremely low, with little expectation for improvement.

Hitler's economic policies broadly matched the political and ideological framework of the Nazi Party itself, the ultimate aim of which was to create an economy that was strong enough to support his foreign policy initiatives. The main facet was a programme of government spending and public investment, which would stimulate demand and expand income. The main beneficiaries of this were the agriculture, building and transportation industries, which saw the biggest expansion in employment. Indeed, by 1939 unemployment had fallen to less than 1%, whilst wages had increased significantly.

However, this dramatic fall in unemployment levels can be at least partially explained by the fact that Hitler significantly reduced the potential labour market by introducing conscription in 1935. Furthermore, even though wages did rise, there was no real improvement in the standard of living as taxation levels also increased to help pay for the government's policies. Indeed, after 1936 the economy was increasingly geared towards rearmament and Hitler's imperialistic, war-like policies.

As Germany's economic recovery developed, many Germans allowed themselves to believe that their country was finally rising from the ashes of their defeat in 1918. This resurgence of national pride gave Germans some purpose and helped fuel Hitler's expansionist policies. As we shall see, every 'desirable' member of German society was given a role to play in achieving this goal.

The use of propaganda

The Nazis were the first to use propaganda and media manipulation to sell their ideology successfully. This helped them to maintain control and to spread their tyranny of beliefs to the German people.

However, recent research suggests that propaganda did not really persuade people to believe in something that they did not want to. Educated middle-class Germans accepted propaganda because it convinced them of attitudes and beliefs that they wanted to hear. Chief among these was that Hitler was saving Germany.

Under Josef Goebbels, the use of propaganda in Nazi Germany became highly sophisticated. Truth was disregarded, and there was a massive emphasis on Nazi ideas and policies, and how Germany was being transformed and reinvigorated by them.

Religion

Hitler believed that control of the churches was important to the maintenance of Nazi authority. As early as 1933 a Concordat or agreement was reached with the Catholic Church, which meant that if the Church did not upset the regime, it would be allowed to continue to preach in Germany.

Protestant churches were put under the control of a Nazi-appointed head of the State Church, called the Reichbishop, who only allowed church ministers who supported the Nazis to continue working.

The Nazi Police State

The Nazi state aimed to totally control all aspects of life in Germany. Nazi Germany was also a totalitarian police state where the power to make and enforce the law and to control the courts was all in the hands of the Nazis.

To understand why Nazi Germany was a totalitarian police state, it is useful to compare its behaviour with that of a democratic society:
- In a democratic society, the police should not take sides in political arguments, but in Nazi Germany the police were ordered to help the Nazis and persecute any opposition to them.
- In a democratic society, people should be free to belong to any organisation they choose, but in Nazi Germany opposition was not tolerated. Just after the Nazis came to power a civil servant resigned his membership of an opposition party saying 'I see no other solution but my resignation. The existence of my family is at stake.' Most non-Nazis in Germany believed that resistance was impossible.
- In a democratic society, judges are meant to make unbiased decisions. In Nazi Germany, judges used Nazi doctrine to direct judgement and sentencing.

- In a democratic society, citizens cannot be arrested unless they have broken a law that has been agreed by an elected parliament. In Nazi Germany, people were kept in prison with no idea of why they were there or when they would be released. This is known as internment without trial. Basic justice was denied to the German population.

Hitler deliberately unleashed a reign of terror with the intention of destroying all opposition and conditioning the rest of the population to obey. It is impossible to exaggerate the role of fear in the Nazi state.

Education and German youth

In schools, young Germans were indoctrinated with Nazi ideals. Particular emphasis was placed on the study of German history, biology and language. However, these subjects were twisted to be consistent with Nazi concepts and were reinforced by Nazi propaganda. Sport also became an important subject, as Hitler believed that healthy bodies were vital for maintaining the racial purity of the German race.

Youth organisations such as the Hitler Youth (*Hitlerjugend*) and the League of German Maidens (*Bund Deutscher Mädel*) were similarly designed to reinforce Nazi doctrine. The intention was, ideologically and physically, to prepare girls for motherhood and boys for military service. As one member recalled, 'we were politically programmed'. German youths were taught that loyalty to the Fatherland overwhelmed everything – thought, deed and action – and were even encouraged to betray their families as a means of service.

> ### The Hitler Youth
> Hitler understood that if his vision of a Thousand Year Reich was to become a reality, he had to indoctrinate the youth of Germany. Consequently, membership of the Hitler Youth was made compulsary for all boys aged between 15 and 18 from 1936 so that they could 'be educated physically, intellectually and morally in the spirit of National Socialism.' Youths were also prepared to take their place in the German Army. By the middle of 1944, members of the Hitler Youth as young as 16 were even being sent to fight on the eastern front against the Soviet Army.

Women

The Nazis believed that the most important roles for women were as mothers and wives. Women were seen as possessions of the State and were chiefly 'employed' as breeding stock for new Nazi generations. As Hitler said in a 1934 speech, 'her world is her husband, her family, her children, and her home.' Women were actively discouraged from taking part in politics and joining the labour force and financial inducements were offered to encourage them to start families. A massive propaganda campaign was launched to further this perception of a woman's role – in 1934, for example, the Mother's Cross was introduced, in bronze for those with four children, in silver (six) and gold (eight), although it was only awarded if the parents were of pure German blood.

Men

Men also had very specific roles manufactured for them and were required to work always for the greater cause of Hitler's vision of a Thousand Year Reich. Men were expected to embody the attributes and ideals of Nazism. This was ideology given flesh, the shape of which was advertised by propaganda posters and films. The perfect 'Nazi-man' was typified by blond hair, blue eyes and a muscular physique, an ideal that, bizarrely, none of the most senior Nazis, including Hitler, resembled!

The Jews

In Nazi Germany, Jews were visible targets who could be blamed for all of Germany's problems. According to Nazi propaganda, Germany had lost World War I because of a Jewish, Communist conspiracy. Jews were also held to be responsible for Germany's economic crises. Hitler offered a scapegoat, or an excuse, to explain Germany's problems and to help non-Jewish Germans feel better about themselves.

The removal of thousands of Jews from their jobs also created vacancies in the labour market, which could be filled by non-Jewish members of the 'master race'. As unemployment fell, Hitler's popularity grew.

During the course of the 1930s, life became intolerable for German Jews. In 1935, for example, laws were passed to prohibit marriages between Germans and Jews. The right to German citizenship was also taken away from Jewish Germans that year. On November 9, 1938, the Nazis organised 'spontaneous' attacks on Jewish synagogues and businesses, causing millions of marks' worth of damage. 91 Jews were murdered and over 20,000 men were arrested and taken to concentration camps. This event became known as *Kristallnacht*. Finally, in January 1939, Hitler predicted in the Reichstag that war would lead to the 'annihilation of the Jewish race in Europe.'

The Holocaust

During World War Two, the Nazis developed the technology and the administrative organisation to murder millions of Jews in Europe. At a cabinet meeting in December 1941, Hans Frank, the Nazi governor of Poland, said, 'Gentlemen, I must ask you to rid yourselves of all feeling of pity. We must annihilate the Jews wherever we find them and wherever it is possible.'

This marked the beginning of the The Final Solution in which the Nazis would attempt to exterminate the entire Jewish population of Europe, an estimated 11 million people. The details of the Final Solution were made clear at the Wannsee Conference on January 20, 1942. When captured, Jews were deported to killing centres. There, immediate death awaited those who were unable to work: the very young, the old, and the weak. Many of the remaining Jews were killed by forced labour with insufficient nourishment. Hundreds of thousands were sent directly to the gas chambers. At Auschwitz, the gas chambers held 2,000 people at a time. With the introduction of a cyanide-based gas called Zyklon B, all 2,000 occupants could be killed in five minutes.

The Nazis also murdered Gypsies, Jehovah's Witnesses, Communists, homosexuals, and the mentally and physically handicapped. However, unlike the Jews, Nazi ideology did not dictate that these groups should be completely wiped out. In principle no Jew was to escape and the suffering of the Jewish people and other groups persecuted by the Nazis did not end until allied armies overran occupied Europe in 1945. By the end of the war, six million Jews had been murdered at the hands of the Nazis.

Why did Germans support the Nazi Party?

As long as the pain of Nazi Germany did not affect most individuals in Germany, they were prepared to go along with the Nazis even if they did not agree with their actions or ideology. Drifting along with something while not actively approving or disapproving of it is called acquiescence.

Most Germans were not active Nazis, but Nazism gave many Germans what they wanted – economic stability and a strong national identity. They were prepared to acquiesce as the Nazi dictatorship spread over all aspects of life in Germany in the 1930s.

Section summary

In this section you should have learned:
- that most Germans accepted the Nazi dictatorship;
- that the Nazis extended their control to all sections of society and all areas of activity;
- that the Nazis established a totalitarian police state;
- how the Nazis destroyed the system of justice, civil rights and individual freedoms.

Practise your skills

'The regime, after all, gave most Germans what they wanted.' How justified is this view of Nazi rule in Germany between 1933 and 1939?

This question is about life in Nazi Germany between 1933 and 1939 and asks how big a part fear and force played in the Nazi control over Germany.

You should **introduce** the main points of your argument – Hitler did provide Germans with jobs and a sense of purpose, but he also destroyed the democratic process and persecuted those who did not follow his ideals. Is it possible that most Germans just acquiesced in Nazi policies and neither supported nor opposed as long as their lives went on relatively unchanged and the Nazis delivered stability?

It is vital in the **main body** of this essay to demonstrate your knowledge of Nazi policies and methods. Do not waffle – be precise and accurate. There are two main sections to deal with in this essay:
- First of all, show what you know about the 'positive' aspects of Nazi rule. What did they do which 'gave most Germans what they wanted'?
- The second section should deal with the use of force and terror – how the Nazis destroyed opposition and used terror tactics to guarantee support.
- Don't forget to mention the role of propaganda in this process!

Remember to start each paragraph with a key sentence which outlines the point you will be developing.

In your **conclusion** you should:
- Decide whether or not you agree with the view expressed in the title. Make your decision clear.
- Sum up the differing points of view and prioritise what you think were the most important features of the Nazi regime within Germany.

One warning. If you get a question about the Nazis in Paper 1, it will focus on either the Nazi rise to power or the Nazi state in Germany up to 1939. You will not get a question about Nazi foreign policy in this paper – that topic is covered in the Road to War special study topic in Paper 2. It might be relevant to mention foreign policy in a Paper 1 essay as a demonstration of how Hitler restored German pride and enhanced his prestige within Germany but do not write too much on it.

Chapter Index

Appeasement and the Road to War, 1933–1939

Introduction

In both the SQA Intermediate 2 and Higher exams, the questions you are asked will be based mainly on sources linked to events between March 1936 and October 1938. However, it is vital that you understand what Appeasement means and also where Appeasement came from. In other words what was the background to Appeasement? To answer that question you must know the key events and developments between the end of World War I in 1918 and the remilitarisation of the Rhineland in March 1936.

What was Appeasement?

> ## At a glance
> This section defines Appeasement and shows the problems of achieving its aims.

Appeasement was an attempt by the British and French governments to 'appease' (satisfy) demands made by Hitler and the Italian dictator, Benito Mussolini, in order to prevent war in Europe during the mid to late 1930s.

Most historians accept that the Second World War was caused by German aggression, but some argue that Neville Chamberlain, British Prime Minister from 1937 to 1940, and other supporters of Appeasement were responsible for encouraging Hitler's aggression, which eventually led to the Second World War.

In the 1930s, most of the British government and the public seemed to support the policy – but perhaps what they really supported was anything that would avoid war. Appeasement was meant to avoid war, but Britain declared war on Germany on September 3, 1939. Appeasement failed.

What is meant by the term 'Appeasement'?

Appeasement was a policy of negotiation intended to solve genuine grievances arising from the peace treaties after World War I. The aim was to remove the possibility of conflict.

Here are some 'opinions' about Appeasement:

An opinion from a supporter of Appeasement might sound like this:

> 'Appeasement was the only sensible policy, given the public's attitude towards war in the 1930s, Britain's lack of readiness to fight and the fact that Britain had no reliable allies to help.'

An opinion from an opponent of Appeasement might sound like this:

> 'Appeasement was a policy of cowardice. It meant giving bullies whatever they wanted and hoping they would not ask for anything more . . . but they always did.'

Appeasement during the 1930s was controversial. Not everyone supported it, despite what the government and its supporters in the press wanted people to think. Since World War Two, the policy of Appeasement has been a source of debate amongst historians.

> ## Section summary
> In this section you should have learned:
> • that Appeasement was the name of a policy adopted by Britain in the late 1930s;
> • why the policy of Appeasement has remained controversial ever since.
>
> These ideas are vital to an understanding of this section of the course. If you are unsure about them go back to your Sources of Information (SOI). These can refer to your notes and class materials, textbooks and videos used or websites visited – in fact, anything you use which gives relevant information about the topics studied. Use any gaps in your knowledge to your advantage. They will provide a focus for further revision or as questions to ask your teacher/tutor about.

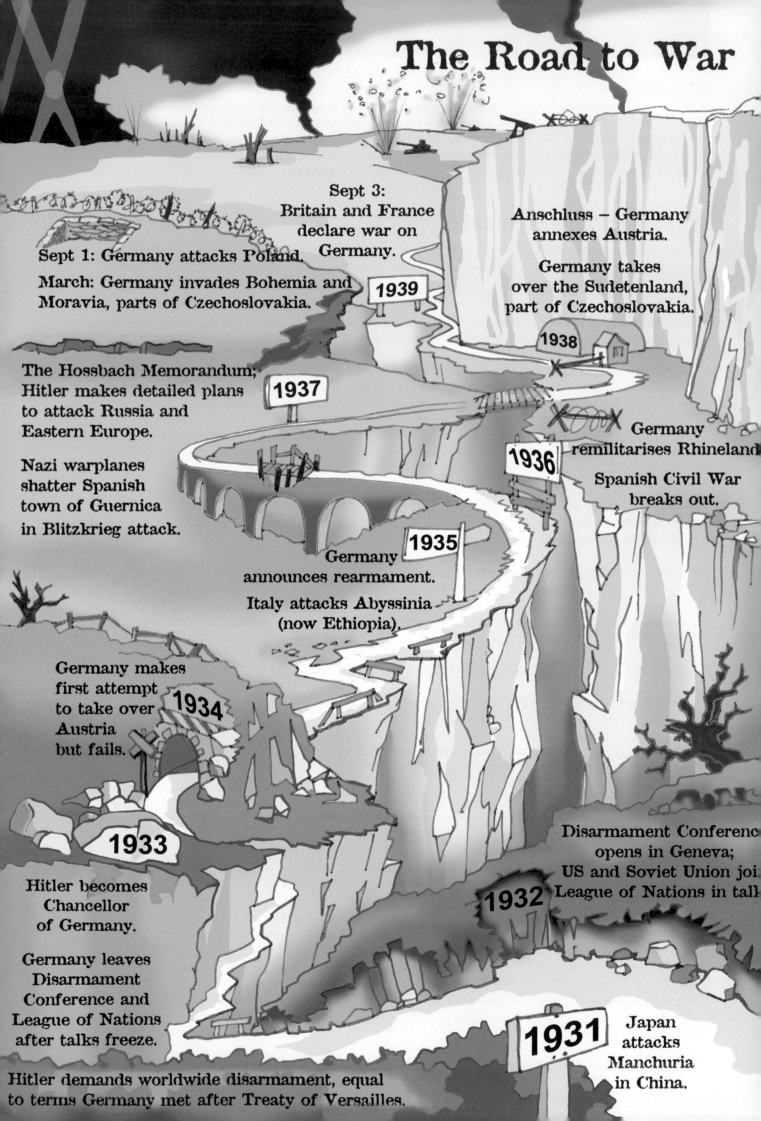

The Road to War

Sept 3: Britain and France declare war on Germany.

Sept 1: Germany attacks Poland.

March: Germany invades Bohemia and Moravia, parts of Czechoslovakia.

1939

Anschluss – Germany annexes Austria.

Germany takes over the Sudetenland, part of Czechoslovakia.

1938

The Hossbach Memorandum; Hitler makes detailed plans to attack Russia and Eastern Europe.

Nazi warplanes shatter Spanish town of Guernica in Blitzkrieg attack.

1937

Germany remilitarises Rhineland.

Spanish Civil War breaks out.

1936

Germany announces rearmament.

Italy attacks Abyssinia (now Ethiopia).

1935

Germany makes first attempt to take over Austria but fails.

1934

1933

Hitler becomes Chancellor of Germany.

Germany leaves Disarmament Conference and League of Nations after talks freeze.

Disarmament Conference opens in Geneva; US and Soviet Union join League of Nations in talks.

1932

1931 Japan attacks Manchuria in China.

Hitler demands worldwide disarmament, equal to terms Germany met after Treaty of Versailles.

The Treaty of Versailles

Syllabus relevance
Background for Intermediate 2 and Higher.

At a glance
The Treaty of Versailles, signed in June 1919, was meant to ensure that Germany would never again threaten the peace of Europe. Instead, most Germans were furious about the Treaty. Tensions created by it partially led to the Second World War 20 years later.

The First World War ended in 1918. It became known as 'the war to end all wars' because people were determined that there should never be another war. So what went wrong? Why was there a Second World War?

The Treaty of Versailles is a vital starting point for studying the path to World War Two. Appeasement came to mean the willingness of Britain and France to allow Germany to break or alter the terms of the Treaty.

The Treaty of Versailles
In 1919, the victorious allies made Germany sign the Treaty of Versailles.

- Germany was forced to accept blame for causing the war and all the death and destruction that resulted from it. This became known as the War Guilt Clause.
- Germany lost all its colonies, much of its industrial resources and areas of land to neighbouring countries including Poland, France, Belgium and Denmark.
- Germany's armed forces were severely cut. It was not allowed any aircraft, tanks or submarines. Limits were placed on the size of its navy. Its army was cut to 100,000 men.
- Most of the western frontier of Germany, called the Rhineland (including the Saar), was demilitarised, which meant that no German troops were allowed in the area. The intention was to make it impossible for Germany to launch a surprise attack into Belgium and France as it had done in 1914.
- Germany also had to pay reparations (compensation) to the victorious powers.

Most Germans were furious. They called the treaty a *Diktat* – a dictated treaty that was forced on them. Much of Nazi foreign policy in the 1930s was based on breaking the Treaty of Versailles in order to re-establish the nation as a strong, influential country.

How Germany was affected by the Treaty of Versailles

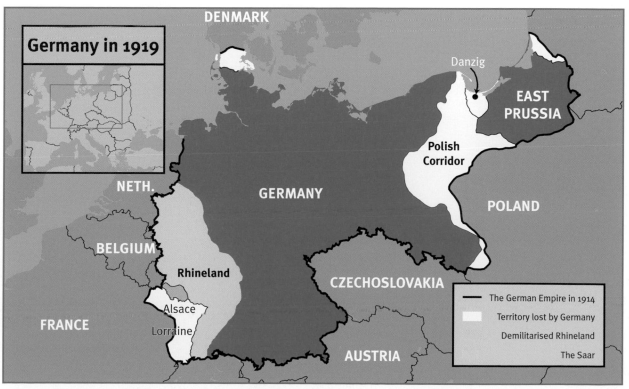

There is no doubt that the harshness of the Treaty of Versailles was a major contributor to the political situation in Europe during the 1930s:

- The Treaty provided a popular target for Hitler to attack during his rise to power.
- The British view that the Treaty's conditions were too harsh was a reason why no action was taken against Hitler during the mid 1930s.
- France wanted to prevent any changes to the Treaty and disagreements between France and Britain over how to deal with Germany prevented combined action.
- Hitler could claim his actions in the 1930s were merely demands for 'fair treatment'.

Other World Events in . . .

1919 In the USA, the Eighteenth Amendment of the Constitution is passed, beginning the era of Prohibition and banning the manufacture and sale of alcohol in the country.

On March 23, Benito Mussolini founds his fascist political movement in Milan, Italy.

The Third Anglo-Afghan war begins. Britain is defeated in 1921, giving Afghanistan complete independence for the first time in its history.

Palestinian-Arab nationalism is born in reaction to a British promise to aid the establishment of a Jewish state in Palestine.

Section summary

In this section you should have learned that:
- the Treaty of Versailles was meant to guarantee that Germany would never again threaten peace in Europe;
- the Treaty of Versailles is connected to the causes of World War Two;
- the Treaty of Versailles left Germany bitter and wanting revenge;
- the Treaty led to difficulties between France and Britain.

These ideas are vital to an understanding of this section of the course. If you are unsure about them, go back to your SOI. Use any gaps in your knowledge to your advantage. They will provide a focus for further revision or as questions to ask your teacher/tutor about.

Practise your skills

Defeat in World War I led to shame and bitterness being felt throughout Germany. The following extract is from the German newspaper, *Deutsche Zeitung*, sold on June 28, 1919.

Vengeance!

German nation!

Today in the Hall of Mirrors at Versailles, a disgraceful treaty is being signed. Never forget it! Today, German honour is dragged to the grave. Never forget it! The German people will push forward to reconquer their place among the nations of the world. There will be vengeance for the shame of 1919.

Your task

How does this source suggest that there is a link between the end of World War I and the outbreak of World War II? Write about half a page.

Select as many relevant quotes as you can from the source and then develop each one by explaining what they mean and their relevance to your main task.

Remember to sum up your answer with a conclusion giving an overall answer to the main question.

You should have noted the following points:
- The source talks about revenge.
- The revenge is for the Treaty of Versailles which is called 'the shame of 1919'.
- It refers to the disgrace caused by the Treaty – 'German honour is dragged to the grave'.
- It is an aggressively worded article that states Germans must 'reconquer their place'.
- Finally it states: 'There will be vengeance'.

Overall conclusion: Make the point that the source comes from 1919 and was, in its own way, predicting the future. It did not have the benefit of hindsight.

Honesty check
If you didn't include these points do you now understand them? If not, use these gaps in your knowledge as points to revise or to ask your teacher/tutor about.

The League of Nations – The Guardian of Peace?

Syllabus relevance
This is background for both Intermediate 2 and Higher.

At a glance
The League of Nations began its life on January 20, 1920 and was based in Geneva, Switzerland. Its aim was to ensure that there would be no repeat of World War I. The League of Nations intended to ensure world peace through a combination of Disarmament and Collective Security. Both these methods failed. It can be argued that Appeasement grew out of the failure of the League of Nations.

In the 1930s the League failed to stop the drift to war. Why?

The League of Nations was not a League of **ALL** Nations
Amongst the original 42 members of the League of Nations were Argentina, Australia, Cuba, France, Italy, Japan, Persia, Switzerland, South Africa, the United Kingdom and Yugoslavia. However, the United States refused to join, whilst Soviet Russia and Germany were not allowed to join at first and consequently saw it as an organisation to protect the interests of the victors of World War I. Japan left the League in the early 1930s, as did Germany. Italy also left in 1935. By the 1930s, 'League action' really came to mean what the remaining major powers – Britain and France – would do in response to any particular international issue.

It was too idealistic
The League made certain assumptions about the future – for example, that all countries would want to be democratic and peace-loving. But what would happen if disarmament didn't happen and collective security didn't work? What would happen if countries were not democratic and peace-loving? That is exactly what happened in the 1930s.

The main members of the League chose self-interest before collective security
The British public expected 'the League' to sort out problems. But what was the League? The League was only as strong as its member countries. Any action on behalf of the League would involve Britain. Would the British public accept British soldiers fighting and dying in the cause of 'peace' if it was not a vital British interest? Politicians worried about the cost of action and its impact on votes.

Section summary
In this section you should have learned:
- why the League was started;
- how it was meant to keep the peace;
- why there were serious doubts, even in the 1920s, about the likely effectiveness of the League.

These ideas are vital to an understanding of this section of the course. If you are unsure about them go back to your SOI. Use any gaps in your knowledge to your advantage. They will provide a focus for further revision or as questions to ask your teacher/tutor about.

The Failure of the League

Part 1 – The failure of Disarmament

Syllabus relevance

Background only for Intermediate 2 and Higher.

At a glance

After World War I, there were hopes that international disarmament would prevent war happening again, but hopes for disarmament had collapsed by 1934.

The failure of Disarmament

Disarmament would only work if countries trusted each other, but that was unlikely in the years following World War I. One of the main obstacles to disarmament was the attitude of France. Throughout the 1920s and early 1930s, the French position towards disarmament was summed up by their attitude that they would not reduce their weapons until Germany dropped their alleged desire for revenge and the destruction of the Treaty of Versailles.

By the mid 1920s, France planned a defensive policy based on a vast line of defences along the Franco-German border called the Maginot Line. France also made a series of alliances with central European countries such as Poland and Czechoslovakia.

On the other hand, Britain saw the French as being particularly unreasonable towards the Germans and refused to support French policy. Britain wanted to stay out of Europe as much as possible.

In 1925, at the Treaty of Locarno, Germany accepted much of the Versailles settlement including the land losses to France and Belgium and the demilitarised Rhineland. It seemed as if a source of international bitterness had been removed. However, Germany said nothing about its eastern frontiers with Poland or Czechoslovakia and so France remained suspicious about what Germany was planning in the east. Britain had made it clear that it was not concerned about what happened in eastern Europe. In such an atmosphere, France was not likely to discuss disarmament.

Other World Events in the . . .

1920s

In 1922, the militant arm of the Sinn Fein Party forms the Irish Republican Army (IRA).

In 1922, the tomb of King Tutankhamen is unearthed in the Valley of the Kings, Egypt.

In 1924, Lenin dies. By 1926, Joseph Stalin has established himself as dictator of the USSR.

In 1925, Scotsman John Logie Baird gave the first demonstration of the television.

In 1926, AA Milne publishes his first book about Winnie the Pooh and his friends.

By 1934, disarmament and the hopes of the League had faced serious setbacks:
- Militarism and fascism were growing, and at the same time the democracies were weak and divided.
- The Disarmament Conference of 1932–33 had broken up with no agreement reached after Hitler declared that the plans for disarmament treated Germany unfairly.
- Germany had left the League of Nations and Hitler had risen to power promising to destroy the Treaty of Versailles.
- Britain hoped to appease Hitler and in so doing tempt him back into the League.
- France was fearful of German growth and was against any Appeasement of Germany.
- In the Far East, Britain had angered Japan by ending their alliance and trying to limit the size of the Japanese navy.

Section summary

In this section you should have learned that:
- countries were meant to disarm in the years after World War I;
- disarmament depended on trust and cooperation;
- hopes for disarmament had collapsed by 1934;
- the failure of the Disarmament Conference meant that a key aim of the League had failed.

These ideas are vital to an understanding of this section of the course. If you are unsure about them go back to your SOI. Use any gaps in your knowledge to your advantage. They will provide a focus for further revision or as questions to ask your teacher/tutor about.

Part 2 – The failure of Collective Security

> ### Syllabus relevance
> Background only for Intermediate 2. Important for Higher.
>
> ### At a glance
> In the 1930s, collective security failed because members of the League of Nations were not prepared to get involved in issues outwith their own national interest. Once the League's 'bluff' of collective security was called, it had no chance of preserving the peace. The weaknesses of the League were exposed in two crises – one in Manchuria and the other involving Abyssinia.

What is Collective Security?

The League had no single army to enforce its decisions. Pressure from the League was only possible if member states agreed to join together to carry out the sanctions, or punishments, agreed by the League members. In other words, members of the League of Nations agreed to work together (collectively) to guarantee their collective peace and security.

Manchuria, 1931

The first test of collective security came in 1931 when Manchuria, which was part of China, a League member, was attacked by another League member (Japan). Collective Security failed to stop the attack or punish the aggressor.

It is not necessary to know the details of the Japanese invasion of Manchuria for this course but it is important to be aware that the Manchurian crisis was the first test for the League – and the League failed. Although Japan was condemned by the League, Japan simply ignored it and carried on attacking China.

> ### Other World Events in . . .
> ### 1931
> The League of Nations criticises Poland for the mistreatment of a German minority in Upper Silesia.
>
> King Alfonso XIII of Spain is overthrown and a Republic is declared.
>
> Chicago gangster Al Capone, who controls the city's illegal alcohol supplies, is found guilty of income tax evasion.
>
> The Empire State Building in New York is opened.

Italy, Abyssinia and the beginnings of Appeasement

The Italian invasion of Abyssinia in 1935 was the second important test for collective security. It was significant because it showed the inability of the League of Nations to stop a country that was determined to use force to achieve its aims. It showed that the 'Pillars of the League' – Britain and France – put self-interest before collective security.

Why did Britain and France fail to support the League?

Britain and France saw Mussolini as an important ally against Hitler. In 1935, Italy, Britain and France had formed the Stresa Front as a way of restricting the growth of Hitler's Germany. However, the Abyssinian crisis split the Stresa Front. When Italy attacked Abyssinia, it was clearly in the wrong. As the main powers in the League, Britain and France should have enforced the League's rules. However, Britain and France appear to have thought it was more important to keep Italy 'on side' as an ally against Hitler.

The Crisis over Abyssinia

On October 7, 1935, the League of Nations condemned Italy for attacking Abyssinia. According to the League Covenant (its rules), Italy should be punished for attacking Abyssinia. But how would Italy react if Britain and France imposed sanctions such as banning oil exports to Italy? Mussolini had made it clear that oil sanctions would be seen as an act of war against Italy.

Britain's military leaders believed that Britain could not defeat Italy quickly. More importantly, any conflict in the Mediterranean Sea area would threaten Britain's route to its Empire in India and the Far East (see map on page 65).

The Hoare-Laval Plan

Britain and France were in a difficult position. Their solution was the Hoare-Laval Plan (Samuel Hoare and Pierre Laval were the Foreign Ministers of Britain and France respectively) which was intended to 'buy off' Italy with the offer of territory in north-east Africa, some of it Abyssinian, on condition that Italy stopped its war. It looked as if Italy was about to be rewarded for its aggression.

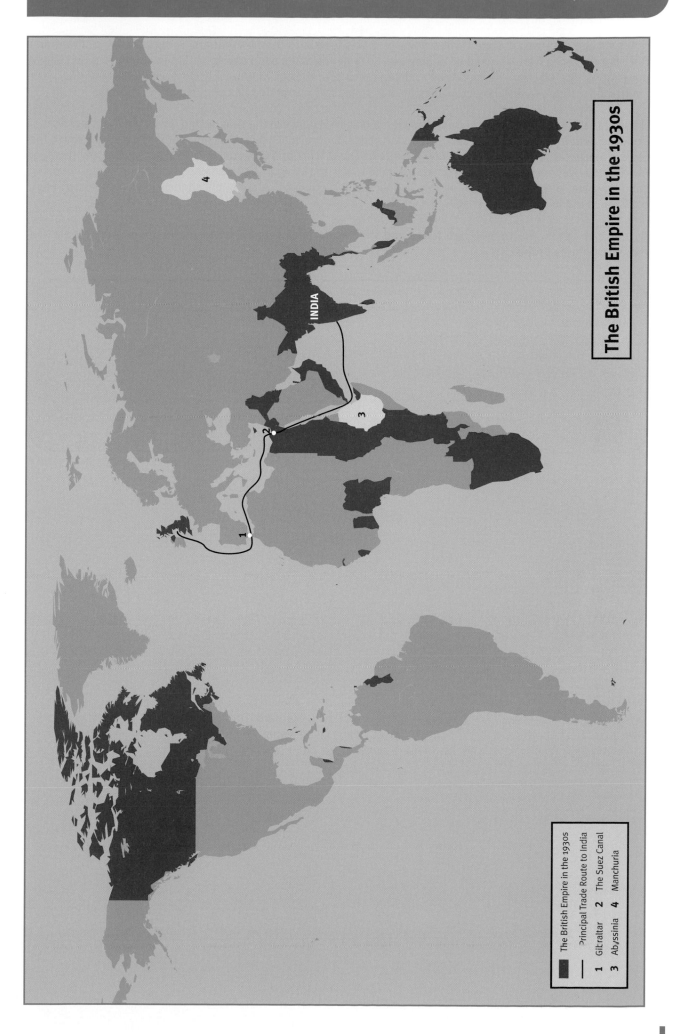

The British Empire in the 1930s

INDIA

The British Empire in the 1930s
Principal Trade Route to India
1 Gibraltar 2 The Suez Canal
3 Abyssinia 4 Manchuria

However, the plan was dropped when news of it was leaked to the newspapers. A big scandal followed and Britain and France were accused of 'selling out' League principles and putting self-interest before their League obligations. The Abyssinians continued to defend their country, but without support from the League they were no match for Italy's tanks and aeroplanes. In May 1936, Italy completed its conquest of the country.

News of the Hoare-Laval Plan destroyed any remaining confidence in the League and it was the first clear sign of Appeasement in action. Indeed, many historians consider the crisis over Abyssinia to be the rock on which the League was wrecked. Historian AJP Taylor wrote in *The Origins of the Second World War* that the real death of the League was in December 1935. He explained that the League had seemed a powerful body imposing sanctions one day, but by the next day it had lost its influence. After publication of the Hoare-Laval Plan, confidence in the League vanished.

By the mid 1930s, the League had failed and this failure is closely linked to the adoption of the policy of Appeasement by Britain.

Section summary

In this section you should have learned:

- what was meant by collective security;
- why the crises in Manchuria and Abysinnia were so important for the League of Nations;
- why the Hoare-Laval Plan signalled the death of the League.

These ideas are vital to an understanding of this section of the course. If you are unsure about them go back to your SOI. Use any gaps in your knowledge to your advantage. They will provide a focus for further revision or as questions to ask your teacher/tutor about.

Practise your skills

Here's a question for you to try. It is not an exam-type question since those on the Road to War topic will be based on sources. However, this is a useful review exercise that makes you organise your knowledge and thoughts about events which led to the adoption of Appeasement as British policy by the mid 1930s. The information required to answer this question is directly relevant to questions you could be asked about in the exam.

Review question
'The aims and methods of the League were seriously damaged between 1931 and 1935.' Do you agree with this statement?

Use the rules of essay writing from Paper 1 – remember **Topic** and **Task**.
- The topic of this question is the League of Nations – its aims, its methods and the crises it faced between 1931 and 1935.
- The task is to consider whether or not the crises had seriously damaged the League of Nations by 1935.

Your **introduction** should establish the aims of the League and its methods.
- The main aim was to keep peace.
- The methods were to be Disarmament to reduce international suspicion and Collective Security.
- Indicate that you will show how these aims and methods had been discredited by 1935 with the failure of the Disarmament Conference and the crises in Manchuria and Abyssinia.

The **main body** of your essay must develop the ideas in your introduction. The following main points should be expanded to demonstrate your detailed knowledge:
- The Disarmament Conference, which met between 1932 and 1933, ended in disagreement and suspicion.
- In 1931 Japan, a League member, attacked Manchuria in China, another League member. Sanctions and collective action were not effective.
- By the end of 1935, not only had Italy used aggression against another League member in Abyssinia, but Britain and France, the main powers in the League, seemed to be betraying League principles by setting up the Hoare-Laval Plan.

Your **conclusion** should sum up your main ideas and answer the main question set:
- You should make the point that, by the end of 1935, the means of guaranteeing security through the League were shown to be ineffective and countries started to look for some other way of protecting their interests.
- It was therefore true that by 1935 the main aims and methods of the League had failed. Conflict was increasing and the machinery of the League seemed incapable of stopping it.

Hitler's Foreign Policy

Hitler's Foreign Policy Aims

You must have an understanding of what Hitler's foreign policy was in order to make sense of his moves between 1935 and 1939 . 'Foreign policy' means more than the way that Hitler dealt with other countries and how he made Germany stronger. It also refers to how his different actions and policies fitted into an overriding plan which had exact targets. Nearly all of Hitler's actions can be linked to four key aims which he had outlined in his autobiography *Mein Kampf* (My Struggle), written during his time in prison in the mid 1920s.

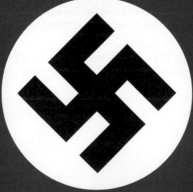

'We must have revenge for the humiliation of Versailles.'

'We Germans are the master race. We have the right to make other races our servants. They are not our equals.'

'We must make Germany strong by bringing together all German-speaking people in one large country.'

'As Germany grows more powerful, we must have land and resources so that Germans can have space to live in and grow strong.'

What were Hitler's aims?

1. The Treaty of Versailles had to be destroyed
    The Treaty symbolised Germany's humiliation. Most of what happened later can be directly linked to Hitler's aim of destroying the Treaty of Versailles.

2. Hitler wanted all German-speaking people to live in one enlarged Germany
    He said that all Germans had the right to live in Germany and if that meant the country's borders had to expand to accommodate them, then he was prepared to make that happen.

3. Germans were the master race
    Hitler believed Aryans – or Germans – were the master race and talked about 'inferior' races such as Jews and Slavs as sub-humans – not even real people. The Nazi word for sub-humans was *Untermenschen*. Hitler believed the *Untermenschen* had one purpose in life – to serve the master race.

4. Hitler wanted *Lebensraum* (Living Space)
    Hitler believed that Germany was defeated in World War I partly because it ran out of resources, especially food and oil. He claimed that Germany had to have all the land and resources it needed to survive and grow strong, even if it meant taking these things from other countries, especially Russia, Hitler's ultimate *Lebensraum* goal.

    > **The Third Reich**
    > One of Hitler's key aims was the creation of a Third Reich (or 'Empire'), which would last for a thousand years. Hitler wanted to restore Germany to the perceived glory of the 'First' Reich – The Holy Roman Empire – and the 'Second' Reich – The German Empire of 1881–1914.

    Hitler's foreign policy was expansionist and potentially aggressive. It's hard to imagine how he could have achieved these aims without planning for war.

Now it's time to see how, or if, Hitler applied these foreign policy aims to what he did in reality.

Section summary
In this section you should have learned:
*   what Hitler's key foreign policy aims were;
*   why Hitler's foreign policy was likely to lead to conflict.

These ideas are vital to an understanding of this section of the course. If you are unsure about them go back to your SOI. Use any gaps in your knowledge to your advantage. They will provide a focus for further revision or as questions to ask your teacher/tutor about.

Hitler rearms Germany, March 1935

Syllabus relevance
Intermediate 2:
> 'foreign policy in practice: rearmament'

Higher:
> 'Attitudes to German rearmament and expansion'

At a glance
The Treaty of Versailles ruled that Germany must have no large warships, military aircraft or submarines, but, in 1935, Hitler announced his intention to rearm Germany. Rearmament meant that Germany not only increased the size of its army but also the size of its navy. Hitler also ordered the creation of a German airforce – the *Luftwaffe*. Between 1933 and 1939, Germany became a much stronger country.

A key point in Hitler's early calculations was the future of the Saarland, an area of Germany close to the Franco-German border rich in iron and coal resources. It had been put under the control of the League of Nations for 15 years, with its coal and iron resources being sent to France as part of Germany's reparations bill. In January 1935, if Germany caused no further problems, a vote – called a plebiscite – would be held in the Saar asking the people there if they wanted to return to German control or not. This is why Hitler did nothing to antagonise Europe before January 1935. He needed the resources of the Saar if Germany was to regain its strength.

In January, the population of the Saarland voted overwhelmingly to return to German rule and soon afterwards, in March, Hitler announced to the world that Germany was rearming.

How did Britain react to German rearmament?
Opinion in Britain was divided about what to do.
- On one hand, some people such as Winston Churchill argued that Hitler was 'moving along the path of war again.'
- On the other hand, it can be argued that Britain encouraged further German rearmament when the Anglo-German Naval treaty was signed in June 1935. In this agreement, Britain accepted the expansion of the German navy, including the use of submarines. Perhaps British politicians believed it was better for Britain to know how big the German navy was, rather than objecting to rearmament but being in no position to stop it.

By the summer of 1935, Hitler had achieved another aim. France was scared of German military growth and made a treaty with Russia. Britain was furious as she distrusted communist Russia. Meanwhile France was angered by Britain's naval deal with Germany. Britain and France, the allies within the Stresa Front, were now divided.

By the end of 1935, Hitler was in a much stronger position
He had regained the resources of the Saarland and successfully started the rearmament of Germany. Hitler had once again broken the terms of the Versailles Treaty and, by provoking a disagreement between France and Britain, had broken the Stresa Front unity. You should also remember that by the end of 1935 Italy had fallen out with its former Stresa friends over the Abyssinian issue.

Section summary
In this section you should have learned:
- why Hitler rearmed Germany;
- how Hitler rearmed Germany;
- why the rearmament issue is an early example of Appeasement in action;
- why Hitler was in a much stronger position by the end of 1935.

These ideas are vital to an understanding of this section of the course. If you are unsure about them, go back to your SOI. Use any gaps in your knowledge to your advantage. They will provide a focus for further revision or as questions to ask your teacher/tutor about.

Practise your skills

As you find out more about Hitler's actions in the 1930s, you will discover that he tended to use two tactics to excuse his actions.

- His first tactic was to confuse and delay international reaction by claiming that Germany was justified in what it did.
- His second tactic was to suggest that if Britain and France let him get away with just one more change in the Treaty of Versailles then he would be happy and peaceful relations could continue.

Now read the following two sources to see those tactics in action.

Extract 1

In 1919, Germany was disarmed and we were given a promise that other countries would also disarm in a few years. How long do we have to wait? Sixteen years have passed since we were made to disarm. Other countries have done nothing. Today, I say to the world that once again Germany will be strong, but only so that we can defend ourselves and also give our people jobs making the weapons we need for our defences.

– Hitler in a speech to the Reichstag, 1935.

Hitler's second tactic can be seen in a statement made on the day that he announced German rearmament in March 1935:

Extract 2

I say this to the leaders of Europe. Yes, we are breaking the treaty but we will get rid of our weapons immediately if other countries do the same. If we are allowed to defend ourselves then we offer a future of peace where all our differences can be discussed peacefully without using force. But if you attack us we will resist to the last man!

Activity

Short essay: *Do you agree that the two statements by Hitler illustrate the tactics mentioned above?*

Your introduction should establish what the tactics mentioned were.
- Read carefully the description of Hitler's tactics.
- You are looking for two different tactics.

Your middle section should link precise source extracts to support your argument.
- For example, the first extract illustrates the justification tactic. Explain how extract 1 does this.
- Move onto the second extract and use 'we will get rid of our weapons immediately if other countries do the same' and also 'if we are allowed to defend ourselves then we offer a future of peace where all our differences can be discussed peacefully without using force.' But don't leave it there. You must now make a clear link between the extracts and which of Hitler's tactics they illustrate.

In your conclusion, answer the question directly and always make sure your 'big answer' follows the theme of the rest of your answer. In other words, don't contradict yourself.

You are now entering the main part of the course!

Advice

In the SQA Intermediate 2 and Higher exams, the sources will be based only on events between March 1936 and October 1938. At Higher, these are:

- Hitler's remilitarisation of the Rhineland
- *Anschluss* with Austria
- Foreign intervention in the Spanish Civil War
- The Czech crisis up to October 1938.

At Intermediate 2 level, the topics are similar but you do not have to cover the Spanish Civil War. However, you do have to cover the Polish crisis up to the outbreak of war, which is not vital at Higher. To be successful in your exam you should be aware of the syllabus. The full course covers 1933 to 1939 and you are expected to be aware 'of the wider context of these events.'

Therefore, although a source is set in March 1936 – or a later date – and is about a specific event within the course syllabus, it is very common for that source to make a reference to earlier events. This allows an examiner to set a question that refers to these events, such as the failure of the League which leads to the issues of Disarmament, Manchuria and Abyssinia and even Hitler's foreign policy.

But don't worry – if you have worked through the book so far, you have covered these points. The next task is an example of the sort of question you could get and also revision of what you have done.

You need to know about the failure of the League with reference to Disarmament, Manchuria and Abyssinia – including the Hoare-Laval Plan.

Activity

Source A expresses many of the views held when Hitler remilitarised the Rhineland in March 1936.

> Last weekend we saw Hitler once again riding roughshod over the terms of the Treaty of Versailles. Where was the League? Where were the brave words of 1919 when we were told World War I was the war to end all wars? The truth is that we are marching towards war again and we cannot hold our heads up when considering the failures of our foreign policy since 1931.

To what extent do you agree with the opinion of Source A that 'we can not hold our heads up . . . since 1931'?

This type of question wants to know what you know about events before the official start of the source questions, which, in the case of Higher level, begins with the Rhineland crisis of March 1936.

To answer this question, start by stating that you agree with the statement by referring to examples of foreign policy embarrassments since 1931, such as:

- The failure to punish Japan over Manchurian aggression
- The failure to stop Mussolini's aggression in Abyssinia
- How the Hoare-Laval Plan 'sold out' the ideals of the League
- The failure of the Disarmament Conference
- How British self-interest led to the Anglo-German naval agreement.

Explain how this information links to the view that British foreign policy had been a failure and shameful – 'we cannot hold our heads up.' It's also a good idea to show that you can think about a question rather than just list information. A point you could make is that British policy was aimed at avoiding wars and maintaining peace. That had been achieved. Could British politicians really have risked taking Britain to war over faraway conflicts in faraway places?

In your conclusion you can offer a balanced opinion. The League seemed to have failed, but the ultimate end of British policy – protecting British interests and maintaining peace had been achieved. So is it fair to talk about: 'the failures of our foreign policy since 1931'?

Honesty check

If you didn't include these points do you now understand them? If not, use these gaps in your knowledge as points to revise or to ask your teacher/tutor about.

The Remilitarisation of the Rhineland

Syllabus relevance

Intermediate 2:
> 'foreign policy in practice: reoccupation of the Rhineland'

Higher:
> 'the interaction of Nazi foreign policy and the policy of Appeasement, as seen through the reoccupation of the Rhineland'

At a glance

The Treaty of Versailles had demilitarised the Rhineland. This meant that no German soldiers were allowed in or near the Rhineland. Be careful about that point. The Rhineland was part of Germany and had NOT been taken away at the Versailles settlement. Hitler did not invade the Rhineland. On March 7, 1936, Hitler simply sent German soldiers back into it. Hitler knew that remilitarisation broke both the Treaty of Versailles and the Treaty of Locarno. Britain and France took no action against Hitler. Why not?

This is the first section that is specifically examined in Paper 2. It is highly likely that you will be given a source that refers to the remilitarisation of the Rhineland.

You must know:
- Where the Rhineland is (refer to the map on page 59 if you aren't sure)
- Why it was demilitarised
- What happened to it in March 1936
- Why Germany was not stopped from remilitarising the Rhineland.

A demilitarised Rhineland meant that Germany's western border was open to French invasion. Before Hitler started his eastwards expansion he needed a secure western frontier. When Hitler reoccupied the Rhineland with German soldiers he was taking a gamble. The League of Nations had been set up partly to supervise the terms of Versailles and, as the main members of the League, Britain and France should have taken action against Hitler. His military leaders had told him not to remilitarise the Rhineland since the German army was in no position to fight if they had to face any opposition. But Hitler's gamble paid off.

British and French responses to the remilitarisation of the Rhineland

Britain and France did nothing about the remilitarisation of the Rhineland for very different reasons.

The British position

Britain was angered by the French alliance with the USSR, signed in 1935. The British felt that Hitler had some justification in claiming that remilitarisation was a defensive move to balance the threat on two fronts from Russia and France.

By 1936 many people believed that Germany had been treated too severely at Versailles. As Lord Lothian said, the Germans are 'only moving troops into their own back garden.' Remember remilitarisation was not an invasion or an attack.

Britain also hoped in 1936 that if she appeased Germany over the Rhineland, Germany would re-enter the League and start talking again about disarmament. Hitler even promised a 25 year peace agreement if he was allowed to remilitarise the Rhineland!

If Hitler was removed from power what would replace him? The British government feared the spread of Communism and there was a saying at the time – 'better Hitlerism than Communism.'

There was a very strong anti-war feeling in Britain. Could any politician justify sending British troops to attack Germany, when Germany had attacked no other country?

The French position

France remembered with bitterness the consequences of its invasion of the Ruhr when it was left standing alone apart from Belgium and condemned by most of the world (see page 42). France would not take solo action again.

Within France, there were political divisions which had already led to serious rioting in Paris. A conflict with Germany could plunge France into political chaos.

French military leaders advised no action against Germany. They believed Germany was stronger than it really was.

France had spent almost its entire military budget on the Maginot Line – a huge line of fortifications, much of it underground. The French felt safe behind their Maginot line, described by one observer as 'an expensive hidey-hole'. French military planning was defensive, summed up as 'the Maginot Mentality'. Any action against Germany in the Rhineland would have entailed leaving the Maginot Line, and the French had not planned for any offensive action against Germany.

What were the Consequences of the Remilitarisation of the Rhineland?

Hitler effectively 'locked the door' on the western frontier of Germany. Hitler started to build a line of fortifications along the German/French frontier called the Siegfried Line. The German public and military commanders were happy; Hitler felt politically safer and he could turn his attention to eastward expansion and *Lebensraum*.

Section summary

In this section you should have learned:
- why the Rhineland had been demilitarised;
- why Britain and France should have taken action against Germany;
- why Germany was not stopped from remilitarising the Rhineland;
- how the remilitarisation of the Rhineland fits into the course about Appeasement and the Road to War.

These ideas are vital to an understanding of this section of the course. If you are unsure about them go back to your SOI. Use any gaps in your knowledge to your advantage. They will provide a focus for further revision or as questions to ask your teacher/tutor about.

Practise your skills

In both the Intermediate 2 and Higher exam, it is likely that you will have to answer a question based on a cartoon. Here is an example of how to tackle such a question.

The following cartoon, called 'The Goose-Step' is one piece of evidence about how some people in Britain felt at the time. It was published in the British magazine *Punch*.
Below the cartoon is written the short verse:
> Goosey Goosey gander,
> Whither dost thou wander? [Where are you going?]
> Only through the Rhineland –
> pray, excuse my blunder.

THE GOOSE-STEP.

"GOOSEY GOOSEY GANDER,
WHITHER DOST THOU WANDER?"
"ONLY THROUGH THE RHINELAND—
PRAY EXCUSE MY BLUNDER!"

In the Higher exam, the wording of a cartoon question is likely to contain the words 'comment on the significance of the cartoon in the light of events at the time'. This means that you have to do three things:

1. Set the cartoon in context by explaining the events that caused the cartoonist to draw that particular cartoon.
2. Pick out as many points from the source as you can which are relevant.
3. Explain the meaning of the points selected.

Now try it for yourself.

Activity

Comment on the significance of the cartoon in the light of events at the time.

You should start by describing briefly the events that caused the cartoonist to draw the cartoon. This is called placing the carton in context and you could write something like this:

> This cartoon refers to the remilitarisation of the Rhineland, ordered by Hitler in March 1936. The remilitarisation broke the terms of the Treaties of Versailles and Locarno. It was another challenge to the Treaty of Versailles.

You could then go on to explain the meaning of the points in the cartoon. Don't just describe the cartoon. When you mention something in it, explain what point the cartoonist is making. Here are some examples of the sort of points you should be making when answering a question based on this cartoon.

1. The German army remilitarised the Rhineland, hence the goose carrying lots of weapons.
2. The title of the cartoon is also significant since the goose-step was the name given to the style of marching used by the German army.
3. Remilitarisation was extremely popular with Germans who welcomed the German troops, hence the welcoming flags hanging from the windows.
4. Hitler said he had no warlike motives for the action, hence the olive branch which is a symbol of peace.
5. The words *Pax Germanica* are difficult if you don't know Latin. The label means 'the German peace' but did that mean there would be peace, but only on Germany's terms?
6. The most important word in the poem is 'only'. Hitler argued that the remilitarisation of the Rhineland threatened nobody. Was it really so important by 1936, when so many other terms of Versailles had been changed?
7. Watch out for irony in cartoons. Don't always take the words in a cartoon at face value. This cartoon is British. The ripped up Treaty of Locarno below the webbed foot of the goose shows that Britain was well aware that Hitler had broken international agreements and the word 'only' might be included ironically, suggesting that if Hitler gets away with this, he might want more.

Now put this advice to one side and try to write out an answer in your own words which sets the context and uses as many points in the cartoon as possible to explain why remilitarisation was a major issue.

There are seldom more than five marks for this sort of question. You'll get one or two marks for setting the cartoon in context, so if you can pick on four main features of the cartoon and fully explain their relevance and meaning, then you will get full marks.

Practise your skills

Source A is from the leading article of the *Dundee Courier and Advertiser*, March 9, 1936, and refers to Germany's reoccupation of the Rhineland.

> We have yet to learn what the Cabinet thinks about it. But there can be no doubt in the mind of the country. It will refuse to be led into a new world war, to enforce the military clauses of the Versailles Treaty, all the more that they are so manifestly broken now in consequence of the development of French policy.
>
> The plain truth is that the Treaty of Versailles is in tatters, and the responsibility for that is far from being exclusively Germany's. Recriminations over its violation have become worse than a waste of breath. It was an imposed Treaty, valid just as long as the country on which it was imposed remained too weak to resist. That time was passed when Germany recreated her army. If her resurgence was to be resisted it should have been resisted then.

Activity

How fully does Source A reflect public opinion about the remilitarisation of the Rhineland in March 1936?

In the exam, you are likely to get a type of question that will say: 'how fully does this source reflect public opinion about . . .' This is an evaluation question asking if the source gives a fair picture of how people felt and what they thought of events at a particular time.

First of all check where the source comes from and when it was produced. You will find this information in the lines above the start of the source extract. This will give you clues as to what the source is about, if it is official policy, the view of a member of the public or a newspaper's opinion.

You should begin your answer by placing it in context – a good tip for every question. You could prepare introduction outlines for each of the four main events covered by the sources at Higher (check back to page 72 if you are unsure of what these are). In this case, an example is:

This source refers to Hitler's remilitarisation of the Rhineland which took place in March 1936. The remilitarisation broke the terms of the Treaties of Versailles and Locarno.

You used this introduction before for the previous question, but since they are both about the Rhineland in 1936 that's OK. You'll only get one question about any particular topic in the exam so it won't look as if you have prepared it. In a good answer, you should set the source in context and at the same time demonstrate recalled information, so in this example introduction you are already well on your way.

You should then refer to the content. You should quote short extracts from it and then develop them by explaining what they mean. For example: *'The plain truth is that the Treaty of Versailles is in tatters' means that not only did the public feel the treaty had been too harsh, but that it had already been altered – so why fight to prevent changes to a treaty this time?*

You might think there are other points that the source does not mention and which are relevant to the question asked. In that case, write something like *'On the other hand the source does not fully reflect public opinion since there are significant issues not mentioned in the source such as . . .'.*

Try to follow this outline when answering any question about a source. If you do all these things you are meeting the requirements of the question and can expect a good mark.

> ### Honesty check:
> If you find it difficult to write an answer based around these points use that to your advantage by asking your teacher/tutor to help you work on those skills.

The Spanish Civil War and Appeasement

Syllabus relevance

Intermediate 2:
> NONE – The Spanish Civil War is not part of the Intermediate 2 course.

Higher:
> 'the interaction of Nazi foreign policy and the policy of Appeasement, as seen through intervention in the Spanish Civil War.'

At a glance

The Spanish Civil War lasted from 1936 until 1939. Supporters of the legitimate government of Spain were called Republicans. The supporters of the rebels, led by General Franco, were called Nationalists. The war started because of tensions within Spain, but the international importance of the Civil War lies in how it was affected by the actions, or lack of action, of the major European powers.

A brief background to the Spanish Civil War

In 1931, Spain became a republic when the King abdicated. Spain was a country divided between the supporters of the old traditional ways of life and those who wanted to see more social and political reforms. Between 1931 and 1936 the policies of successive governments swung from one extreme to the other and there was no political stability.

In July 1936, General Franco led a military rising to overthrow the recently elected left-wing government in Spain. The military rising turned into a civil war which split the country between the Republicans and the Nationalists. To many outsiders the Spanish Civil War was simplified as a fight between democracy and totalitarian dictatorship.

Other World Events in . . .

1936

The Olympic Games are held in Berlin. Hitler plans to use the Games to show off the strong German economy and to try to prove Aryan physical supremacy by entering a strong German team. Despite the fact that the German team wins the most events, the star of the Games is the Black American Jesse Owens, who wins four gold medals, including the 100m sprint.

In Soviet Russia, Joseph Stalin begins a 'great purge' to kill his enemies. By 1939, over 8 million are dead and perhaps 10 million imprisoned.

In Britain, King George V dies and is succeeded by his son, Edward VIII. Later this year, Edward abdicates the throne so that he can marry American divorcee, Wallis Simpson.

In Scotland, the cartoon strips 'The Broons' and 'Oor Wullie' first appear in *The Sunday Post*.

Foreign Intervention – or lack of it

Soon after the war began, Britain, France, Germany, Italy, Russia and others joined a Non-Intervention Committee. Its purpose was to make sure that there was no foreign intervention in Spain.

Britain was determined not to let the Spanish Civil War grow into a big European war. This policy was known as non-intervention and can be seen as another step in the development of Appeasement.

Neither Britain nor France, who had organised the Non-Intervention Committee, stood up against the interventionist policies of the dictators.

For example, Germany and Italy, key members of the Non-Intervention Committee, broke their promises and sent help to the Nationalist side. Indeed, the German ambassador to Britain in 1937, Joachim von Ribbentrop, said, 'A better name for the Non-Intervention Committee would have been the Intervention Committee.'

Who sent what and why?

The following chart summarises the interventionist – and non-interventionist – policies of the major European powers during the Spanish Civil War.

Who?	What?	Why?
Germany	• German transport planes carried Franco's rebels at the start of the Spanish Civil War • Aircraft – The Condor Legion • Artillery and military observers and advisers	• Spain was a good test for equipment and tactics (eg *Blitzkrieg* and bombing at Guernica) • To entrap France in a Fascist triangle • Spain had reserves of iron ore and tin – necessary materials for war industries • Gratitude from Franco
Italy	• Navy • Soldiers • Tanks • Supported Franco and the Nationalists	• *Mare Nostrum* – 'Our Sea' • Spanish bases would be a balance to British influence at Gibraltar • Prestige – to show off as Mussolini liked 'to wave a big stick'
Russia	• Food at first • Tanks, aircraft and military 'advisers' later • Supported the Republicans	• Cynical use of the war to keep it going • As long as Hitler was distracted in Spain, he would not move against Russia • To test equipment • Stalin did not want to spread Communism – that would anger possible allies against Germany (eg Britain)
Britain	• Did not send any support, although many volunteers fought with the International Brigades	• Britain's policy was Non-Intervention – 'It's not our war' • Opposition to left-wing government • Fear of escalating into European war
France	• Did not send any support	• At first, France wanted to help the Republic – but soon stopped • France would not act without Britain, so also adopted Non-Intervention

What were the International Brigades?

The International Brigades were made up of ordinary people who gave up their jobs and travelled to Spain so that they could make a personal stand against the growth of Fascism in Europe. They were not regular soldiers but were often disillusioned by the weak Appeasement policies of their own democratic governments. There were even Italian and German Communists in the International Brigades who fought Fascist Italian and German troops. Consequently, the Spanish Civil War is sometimes called 'Europe's Civil War'.

In questions about foreign intervention in the Spanish Civil War you will often get two sources. One source usually supports Britain's policy of non-intervention. The other source usually supports the International Brigades. If the writer shows sympathy for the Republic, or refers to his or her own membership of the Labour Party or the Communist Party, then it's a safe bet that the writer opposed the British government's non-intervention policy and supported the International Brigades.

British attitudes to the war

There are four key questions to think about when considering British policy over Spain:

1. Did Britain adopt the policy of non-intervention because the Government was afraid of Nazi and Fascist power?
2. Did Britain feel that it could not take action because more time was needed to re-arm?
3. Did the British government sympathise politically with the aims and values of the rebel Nationalists?
4. Was Britain afraid that a Republican victory would lead to a Communist-controlled Spain?

French attitudes to the war

Viewed from the French perspective, the situation was bleak:

- There was a lack of national unity.
- France regarded the Soviet Union (Russia) as being too far away to be of real practical assistance.
- France was scared about the possibility of a Fascist Triangle surrounding her. With Fascist Italy to the east, Nazi Germany to the north and a fascist Spain to the south, France was faced with the possibility of a three front war if she intervened. This was a nightmare scenario that had to be avoided.

What did European countries learn about each other during the Spanish Civil War?

The German and Italian armed forces appeared to be well-equipped and effective and were ready to support another authoritarian regime. Guernica, a Spanish town, was levelled by bombs dropped by Nazi warplanes. The aircraft were code-named 'the Condor Legion' and revealed to the world that in any future war the bombing of cities would cause massive loss of life.

The British and French seemed to be paralysed. Both countries appeared to lack the resolve or the resources to offer support to the legitimate Spanish government. The confidence of Germany and Italy was boosted.

Stalin now suspected that he could expect no help from Britain and France if the Nazis attacked Russia. Later, the Munich Agreement of 1938 seemed to confirm Stalin's fears and directly led to the Nazi-Soviet Agreement of August 1939 and thereby to World War Two. This is discussed fully on page 95 of this book.

General Franco claimed victory in the Spanish Civil War in March 1939 and led a fascist government in the country until his death in 1975.

Section summary

In this section you should have learned:

- who the Nationalists and the Republicans were;
- why Germany, Italy and Russia got involved in the war;
- why Britain and France adopted a policy of non-intervention;
- why the International Brigades were formed and what they represented;
- why the Spanish Civil War is important within the context of Appeasement and the Road to War.

These ideas are vital to an understanding of this section of the course. If you are unsure about them go back to your SOI. Use any gaps in your knowledge to your advantage. They will provide a focus for further revision or as questions to ask your teacher/tutor about.

Practise your skills

Read the following sources.

Source A is from a letter sent from Spain by Jack Jones of the Labour Party on 9th July, 1938.

> We believe that there can be no compromise between Fascism and Democratic ideals, for which we ourselves have come here to fight. We feel ourselves wholly at one with the determination of the Spanish people to drive out the invaders of their country. As members of the Labour Party, we urge our leaders to turn a deaf ear to talk of compromise, and continue to press ever more vigorously the Party's declared policy; namely, the demand that the British government support of non-intervention be reversed, and that the right be restored to the Spanish Republic freely to purchase arms.
>
> Nothing could be more encouraging to the work of those of us fighting with the British Battalion than to feel that we are being supported by the vigorous efforts of all the Democratic forces of Britain led by the Labour Party. In that struggle, we are proud to act in the advance guard, and pledge ourselves to do all in our power to maintain the high reputation already gained by the Battalion in Spain.

Source B is from a speech at Liverpool by Anthony Eden, MP, Foreign Secretary of the Conservative Government, on 12th April, 1937.

> The policy of non-intervention has limited and bit by bit reduced the flow of foreign intervention in arms and men into Spain. Even more important, the existence of that policy, the knowledge that many governments, despite all discouragement, were working for it, has greatly reduced the risk of a general war.
>
> Six months ago I told the House of Commons of my conviction that intervention in Spain was both bad humanity and bad politics. Nothing that has happened since has caused me to modify that judgment; some events have caused me to confirm it.

Activity

Compare the opinions about intervention in the Spanish Civil War contained in Sources A and B.

This is a source comparison question. For this sort of question you should be able to:
- use content from the source;
- make direct comparisons between the sources;
- credit will be given for recalling any relevant information.

Do not just describe one source then the other. That is not comparison.

Start by showing you understand what the sources are about and place them in context. You could write something like this:

> The sources are both responses to the Spanish Civil War which started in 1936 when General Franco led a military rising against the elected government. The rebels were called the Nationalists and the government side the Republicans.

(This is context, but you will also get marks for recall which means you use your own knowledge to develop your answer.)

Now you should show that you know they have different opinions. Remember you are also asked to compare the sources, so watch out for the comparison points made in this answer:

> One is a left wing point of view by Jack Jones, member of the Labour Party, while the other [comparison] is by Anthony Eden a Conservative MP and the Foreign Secretary, therefore showing government opinion.

The illustrative purpose of the sources differs. Source B supports the policy of non-intervention. It says 'the policy . . . has limited . . . and reduced the flow of foreign intervention in Spain' [content] and 'has reduced the risk of general war' [content]. On the other hand [comparison] Source A says the policy of non-intervention 'should be reversed' [content] and that the Spanish government should be able 'freely to purchase arms' [content]. The non-intervention policy of the British government had denied the Spanish government their legal rights [recall].

In conclusion, the sources differ in attitude because Source A represents a left-wing attitude sympathetic to intervention, and a supporter of the International Brigades [recall], while Source B is a justification of government policy, saying that anything else would be 'bad humanity and bad politics' [content].

Honesty check

If you find it difficult to write an answer based around these points use that to your advantage by asking your teacher/tutor to help you work on those skills.

Anschluss, March 1938

Syllabus relevance

Intermediate 2:
>   'foreign policy in practice: *Anschluss*'

Higher:
>   'the interaction of Nazi foreign policy and the policy of Appeasement, as seen through . . . the annexation of Austria'

At a glance

In March 1938, German troops marched into Austria, in opposition to the terms of the Treaty of Versailles. This event was called *Anschluss*, which means the joining together of Austria and Germany. Britain and France appeased Hitler and did nothing to help Austria.

How did *Anschluss* fit in with Hitler's foreign policy aims?

Hitler wanted to create a 'Greater Germany' by linking German-speaking people together. He wanted to break the Treaty of Versailles and start spreading east as part of his *Lebensraum* plan. (But be careful – don't think that he wanted Austria for *Lebensraum*. Austria was just a stepping stone to that target.)

Early attempts at *Anschluss*

Hitler had already tried to take over Austria in 1934, but he was blocked by Mussolini who threatened to send troops into Austria to prevent Germany taking it over. At that time Mussolini was not a friend of Hitler. Britain and France saw Mussolini as a potential ally against Hitler, which helps explain why they were unwilling to take action against Mussolini when he attacked Abyssinia in 1935. However, after falling out with Britain and France over the Abyssinian crisis and helping the Nationalist side in the Spanish Civil War,

> ### The Hossbach Memorandum
>
> On 5 November 1937, Hitler met with the Commaders-in-Chief of his armed forces, the Reich War Minister and Germany's Foreign Minister to outline his views on the diplomatic situation and the future direction of Germany's foreign policy. Since the end of the war, the minutes of this meeting, recorded by Colonel Hossbach, have been used as evidence to argue that Hitler had decided on and planned the war well before September 1939. Certainly, Hitler did state at that meeting that, by 1943–45 at the latest, Germany must move against Czechoslovakia and achieve *Anschluss* with Austria. However, no mention is made of war against Russia or the establishment of *Lebensraum* in the East.
>
> AJP Taylor has argued that Hitler was only 'day-dreaming' and the fact that subsequent events did not follow the path outlined in this meeting is evidence enough that he was not setting out a 'blueprint' for subsequent German policy. However, other historians have suggested that Hitler knew conflict was inevitable and that the meeting was a clear statement of expansionist intent.

Mussolini became friendlier with Hitler. The Balance of Power had shifted, which meant that Germany was stronger, Britain and France were weaker and Austria was at the mercy of Germany.

Preparations for *Anschluss*, 1938

Between 1934 and 1938, the Nazis kept up the pressure on Austria, most of which was organised by an Austrian Nazi called Arthur Seyss-Inquart. Seyss-Inquart's task was to prepare for a Nazi takeover.

At a meeting in February 1938, Hitler told Kurt von Schuschnigg, the Austrian Chancellor, that Austria could expect no help from Britain and France and that Germany was now allied to Italy, the former protector of Austria. Schuschnigg was scared and returned to Austria hoping to drum up international support. He planned a plebiscite (also called a referendum) to ask the Austrian people if they wanted to be German or if they wanted to stay Austrian. Schuschnigg was gambling that if the Austrians voted to stay separate from Germany, the whole world would know that Hitler had no excuse to invade Austria. The plebiscite was planned for March 13 but Hitler ordered Schuschnigg to call it off, threatening a full-scale German invasion.

Meanwhile Neville Chamberlain, the British Prime Minister said: 'Why should we mislead . . . [small European countries] . . . by giving them an assurance of security when any such security can only be a delusion?'

Faced by the reality that he could expect no help from Britain or France, Schuschnigg resigned. On March 12, 1938, German troops marched unopposed into Austria.

The reaction of Britain to *Anschluss*

The terms of the Versailles agreement were perfectly clear – *Anschluss* was forbidden. However, once again Britain and France did nothing and therefore Austria was annexed and became part of the German Reich.

On March 7, 1938, Chamberlain said:

> 'What small country in Europe today, if threatened by a larger one, can safely rely on the League alone to protect it from invasion? . . . There can only be one honest answer to it, and that is "no-one".'

In this quotation, Chamberlain makes it clear that there was no longer any faith in Collective Security and that apart from Appeasement, he believed there was not much more that could be done.

Opinion in Britain was divided about what to do

Most British people believed that Austria was not their problem and that it was too far away to be given any help. Since many Britons felt that Versailles had been too harsh and since Austria shared a similar culture to Germany, they believed that *Anschluss* was inevitable.

On the other hand, anti-appeasers felt that Hitler was a bully who would keep coming back for more unless he was stopped and that Appeasement just encouraged Hitler's aggression. More practically, politicians such as Winston Churchill felt that *Anschluss* gained Hitler resources, factories, men of military age and control over south-eastern Europe. You'll see more about this in an example question later in this book. However, although Churchill consistently opposed Appeasement, he was not Prime Minister at the time of *Anschluss* and was very much a lonely voice calling in the wilderness.

Section summary

In this section you should have learned:

- Hitler took over Austria in March 1938;
- the German word for linking Germany with Austria is *Anschluss*;
- earlier attempts at *Anschluss* had failed;
- Hitler's relationship with Mussolini is important in the story of *Anschluss*;
- *Anschluss* was an important part of Hitler's foreign policy;
- why Britain decided to appease Hitler.

These ideas are vital to an understanding of this section of the course. If you are unsure about them go back to your SOI. Use any gaps in your knowledge to your advantage. They will provide a focus for further revision or as questions to ask your teacher/tutor about.

Practise your skills

Cartoon analysis

Cartoonists at the time, especially David Low, a consistent opponent of Appeasement, also made it plain how they felt about *Anschluss*.

In this cartoon, originally published in *The Evening Standard*, the person carrying the basket of eggs is meant to be Sir Anthony Eden who was the British Foreign Secretary until his resignation on February 20, 1938. He is saying, 'Why should we take a stand about someone pushing someone else when it's all so far away?'

INCREASING PRESSURE.

David Low/Atlantic Syndication

But Low is being sardonic – he doesn't agree with what Eden said. By portraying him on the edge of a precipice, Low is mocking Eden's statement and suggests that Germany's actions could have a catastophic effect unless Britain does indeed take a stand.

- The context is Hitler's increasing pressure on Austria as part of his expansionist foreign policy.
- Austria is being leaned on, but that is putting pressure on the other countries.
- We can assume the hand pulling the pressure lever is Hitler's and he is using German military strength to exert pressure on Austria.
- The next countries in line, Czechoslovakia and so on, all put pressure on each other and at the end of the line is Britain and France.
- Britain seems more concerned with its Empire (shown as having all its eggs in one basket) but Eden is saying the problem is far away.
- Low is making the point that the pressure will increase and Britain has nowhere to go. Britain is standing on the edge of a precipice and one step back (another yielding to German pressure) could lead to disaster for Britain and France.

Honesty check

If you find it difficult to write an answer based around these points use that to your advantage by asking your teacher/tutor to help you work on those skills.

Another skills practice

Here is another comparison question, this time showing different opinions about *Anschluss*.
The sources are deliberately labelled B and C to remind you to be careful when referring to sources by their identity letter. Don't assume the first source referred to in a question will be A. Do not get source identities mixed up in the exam.

Source B is from a letter to his sister by Lord Tweedsmuir, Governor General of Canada, March 14, 1938.

> I do not myself quite see what there is to fuss about. Austria will be much more comfortable, economically under Germany's wing. That should have been done long ago in the Versailles Treaty. The chief trouble will be if there is any real threat to Czechoslovakia, but there again I think the frontier should be rectified. Surely the Versailles agreement was the most half-witted thing ever perpetrated?

Source C is from a speech by Winston Churchill MP in the House of Commons, March 14, 1938.

> We cannot leave the Austrian question where it is . . . The public mind has been concentrated upon the moral and sentimental aspects of the Nazi conquest of Austria – a small country brutally struck down . . . but there are some things I have not seen brought out in the public press.
>
> Vienna is the centre . . . of all the countries lying to the south east of Europe. A long stretch of the River Danube is now in German hands. The mastery of Vienna gives to Nazi Germany military and economic control of the whole of the communications of south east Europe by road, river and by rail. What is the effect of this upon what is called the balance of power?

Activity

Compare the attitudes towards the German occupation of Austria in March 1938 contained in Sources B and C.

Remember that in a comparison question it is not enough just to describe the two sources. You are asked to compare, so you must pick out points in the two sources where they are similar and points where they differ.

You should first set the source in context:

> Both are reactions to Anschluss in March 1938 when German troops entered Austria against the Treaty of Versailles.

You should then include the following points in your answer:

> The letter by Lord Tweedsmuir (Source B) is to his sister and therefore expresses personal and private opinions, but Source C is part of a speech by Winston Churchill in the House of Commons. Therefore it is a very public and political attack on the policy of Appeasement.

> The sources differ over their attitudes to Anschluss. Source B states, 'I do not myself quite see what there is to fuss about' and says 'Austria will be much more comfortable, economically under Germany's wing', suggesting that Tweedsmuir does not think Anschluss is of great importance. On the other hand, Source C describes it as 'the Nazi conquest of Austria' and claims Austria has been, 'brutally struck down.'

This part of your answer makes a direct comparison and uses content to support your point. The use of the phrase 'on the other hand' makes it clear to a marker that you are comparing (which is what you have been asked to do).

Now make another comparison . . .

Source B shows that Lord Tweedsmuir believes that Anschluss was inevitable since the Versailles settlement was 'the most half-witted thing ever perpetrated,' but failed to see Anschluss as leading to any future problems. Tweedsmuir even believed that Britain should renegotiate the frontiers of Czechoslovakia just to keep the peace – 'The chief trouble will be if there is any real threat to Czechoslovakia, but there again I think the frontier should be rectified'.

On the other hand, Churchill is very worried about the consequences of Anschluss as Nazi strength will increase both militarily and economically. He states, 'The mastery of Vienna gives to Nazi Germany military and economic control of the whole of the communications of south east Europe by road, river and rail' and he wonders, 'What is the effect of this upon what is called the balance of power?'

In conclusion, Source B was written by a supporter of Appeasement, while the author of Source C was very much opposed to it [another comparison point – you should try to identify in comparison questions which one supports Appeasement and which one is against Appeasement].

Honesty check

If you find it difficult to write an answer based around these points, use that to your advantage by asking your teacher/tutor to help you work on those skills.

Czechoslovakia and the Munich Agreement

Syllabus relevance

Intermediate:

'the crisis in Czechoslovakia and the Munich Agreement' also 'attempts to deal with German demands, especially over Czechoslovakia'

Higher:

'the interaction of Nazi foreign policy and the policy of Appeasement, as seen through . . . the developing crises in Czechoslovakia up to Munich'

At a glance

By the summer of 1938, another international crisis erupted, this time over Czechoslovakia. The heart of the crisis was the Sudetenland, a part of Czechoslovakia. The crisis seemed to be solved by an agreement at Munich which is still seen as the classic example of Appeasement in action. Six months later Appeasement as a policy was almost dead when Hitler broke the Munich Agreement.

The background to the crisis

Czechoslovakia was a new country created after World War I. It contained many different nationalities, including three million German speakers who lived in an area called the Sudetenland. In 1938, Europe was close to war because of a crisis over the Sudetenland.

Czechoslovakia was in a very vulnerable position. Nazi-controlled territory bordered western Czechoslovakia to the north, the west and the south.

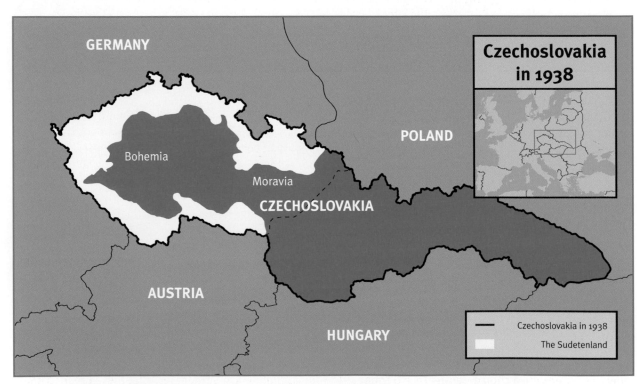

Hitler's ambition of *Lebensraum* meant an eastwards expansion, but Czechoslovakia, with its strong defences, was a barrier to his plans. If Hitler got the frontier area of the Sudetenland, it would be easy to make further advances into Czechoslovakia.

Hitler encouraged the growth of a Sudeten German party led by Konrad Henlein to provoke trouble in the Sudetenland. By August 1938, Hitler was making wild, nationalistic speeches to encourage pro-Nazi demonstrations in the Sudetenland which, Hitler hoped, would cause the Czech police to take strong action. Hitler would then have his excuse to invade, claiming he was protecting the Sudeten Germans from Czech persecution.

By September 1938, Britain was scared. Back in May 1938, Hitler had secretly ordered his army to be ready to attack Czechoslovakia by October 1st. Britain knew about the plan. That deadline provides the reason why there was such desperate activity in September 1938.

The British Prime Minister, Neville Chamberlain, was determined to avoid a war and flew three times to meet Hitler during September 1938. Remembering that air journeys were risky and uncomfortable at that time and that Chamberlain was an old man, you can see that September 1938 really was crunch time for Britain, Appeasement and the chances of peace.

> **Other World Events in . . .**
> **1938** Superman makes his first comic book appearance.
>
> In America, Orson Welles broadcasts HG Wells's *The War of the Worlds* over the radio. Panic ensues as thousands believe that Martians have really invaded New York.
>
> Walt Disney releases his first full-length animated film, *Snow White and the Seven Dwarfs*.
>
> Nestlé finally develops the first instant coffee, after eight years of trying.

Why was Britain involved in the Czech crisis?

Britain was concerned that Czechoslovakia would fight if attacked by Germany. Since France had an alliance with Czechoslovakia, she might fight to help her ally and Britain might also be dragged into the conflict. Britain had no intention of being sucked into a war because of France's alliance with Czechoslovakia – and France had no intention of going to war without British support. Britain and France therefore had to find a way to get 'off the hook'.

Meeting 1 – Berchtesgaden, September 15, 1938

On September 15th, Chamberlain made the first of three visits in two weeks to Hitler. Hitler demanded the Sudetenland at some point in the future. When Chamberlain returned to Britain, he gained the agreement of France and Czechoslovakia for this course of action.

- Chamberlain was pleased because he seemed to have solved the crisis.
- France was relieved because they could now claim they had done their best to secure Czechoslovakia's future.
- Czechoslovakia was left feeling bitter because their ally France had abandoned them and they were forced to agree to hand over their territory.

Meeting 2 – Bad Godesberg, September 22, 1938

A week after the first meeting with Hitler, Chamberlain went into the second meeting confident that the Sudeten problem had been solved. But Hitler had other plans. He was determined to provoke a war and said he wanted the Sudetenland immediately or there would be war. Chamberlain was horrified by Hitler's change of demands. He returned to Britain expecting war to break out and made a BBC radio broadcast to the British public, saying:

> 'How horrible and unbelievable it is that we should be getting ready for war, trying on gas masks and digging air raid shelters in Britain because of a faraway quarrel between people that we know nothing about.'

War was likely. Hitler had demanded a reply from Britain by 2pm on September 28th. The offer of a new meeting, at Munich, came just before 2pm.

Meeting 3 – Munich, September 29, 1938

At the Munich Conference Britain, France, Germany and Italy (which was Germany's ally) met to discuss the future of the Sudetenland. Without consulting Czechoslovakia, which was not even invited to Munich, it was agreed that Germany would occupy the Sudetenland almost immediately. The Chechoslovakian government was now presented with a choice – either face Germany alone or capitulate. On September 30th, they agreed to abide by the agreement.

The Munich Agreement – realism or sell-out?

The Munich settlement is central to any study of Appeasement in the 1930s and quite simply you must know the main points. You should have them in your main sources of information.

To some, the carve-up of Czechoslovakia without consulting the Czech representatives seemed the ultimate sellout of principle. Churchill, for example, described the Munich settlement as 'an unmitigated defeat'.

Letters in the press referred to shock and humiliation over the Munich Agreement and some suggested that Britain had thrown 'Czechoslovakia to the wolves'. However, recent research suggests that Chamberlain manipulated the media to put a positive 'spin' on the Munich Agreement. Yet it is true to say that most of the public preferred to 'sell Czechoslovakia down the river,' as one commentator put it, than risk war with Germany. The majority of the public were pleased that war had been avoided, at least for the time being.

Britain and Germany both agreed to work to improve relations and to avoid war. Hitler was given the Sudetenland as the price of avoiding war and said, 'I have no more territorial demands to make in Europe'. Hitler and Chamberlain also signed an agreement during their private talk at Munich, which resulted in the famous 'piece of paper' that promised 'peace in our time'.

Although it is hard to see Munich as 'Peace with honour', as Chamberlain claimed, perhaps it can be seen as a realistic response to the situation at the time. In the 1960s, historian AJP Taylor claimed that the Munich Agreement was a triumph for British policy. He argued that the policy of Appeasement was not created to save Austria or Czechoslovakia. It was meant to avoid war through negotiation and it successfully did that.

In Britain, most people were greatly relieved that war had been avoided. Few looked to the future implications of such a settlement. The fear of war, especially gas bombing, was enough to make the public glad that peace had been purchased, even temporarily, at some other country's cost.

Once again, David Low captured not only the attitude of the public but also the criticism of British policy over Czechoslovakia in one memorable cartoon.

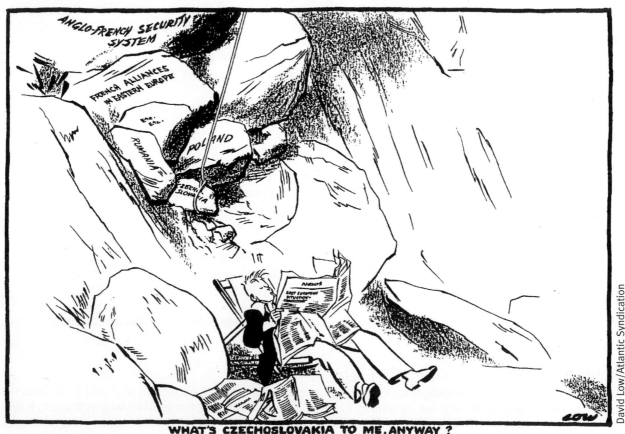

WHAT'S CZECHOSLOVAKIA TO ME, ANYWAY ?

David Low/Atlantic Syndication

The man in the deck chair is meant to be an ordinary British person. He is supposed to be reading about the Czech crisis.

The rope tied to the rocks is presumably being pulled by Hitler. Low suggests that when Czechoslovakia falls it will start a sequence of events that will seriously damage or even destroy Britain – but in 1938 the British public thought it could sit back and forget about 'the faraway country about whom we know nothing' as Chamberlain described it. However, events in March 1939 brought Czechoslovakia right back into the headlines.

Section summary

In this section you should have learned:

- why Czechoslovakia was vulnerable by 1938;
- why the Sudetenland was at the heart of the Czech crisis;
- why Hitler wanted the Sudetenland;
- why Chamberlain flew three times to meet Hitler;
- what the Munich Agreement was;
- why Munich is thought of as the peak of Appeasement;
- why the Munich Agreement is still controversial.

These ideas are vital to an understanding of this section of the course. If you are unsure about them go back to your SOI. Use any gaps in your knowledge to your advantage. They will provide a focus for further revision or as questions to ask your teacher/tutor about.

Practise your skills

Activity

In what ways do the views about Appeasement differ between Source A and Source B?

Source A is from a letter to the editor, signed 'An Ashamed Peace lover', *The Scotsman*, October 1, 1938

> I am sure that on hearing the results of the Munich conference . . . thousands of people will be shocked and humiliated. Czechoslovakia, the victim, had no opportunity of a say in the deliberations which sealed her fate and our Prime Minister, while willing to spend hours with Hitler, has not thought it worthwhile to have any direct talks with Benes [the Czech leader] . . . Britain and France have shown that they are not willing to fight for Czechoslovakia but they are willing to hand over her industry, property etc. to Hitler as it stands.
>
> Britain and France appear to have thrown Czechoslovakia to the wolves.

Source B is from *Why England Slept* by John F Kennedy, 1940

> I believe that Chamberlain was sincere in thinking that a great step had been taken towards healing one of Europe's fever sores. . . Most people in Britain felt, 'It's not worth a war to prevent the Sudeten Germans from going back to Germany'. They failed at that time to see the larger issue, involving the domination of Europe. But although all these factors played a part in the settlement of Munich, I feel that Munich was inevitable on the grounds of lack of armaments alone.

Points to make

When you summarise the content of sources you should always explain what was happening which caused the sources to be produced – this is called putting the sources in context.

You should start your answer by identifying that both sources refer to the Munich Agreement, which dealt with the future of the Sudetenland in Czechoslovakia. Make it clear that you understand the sources differ over their attitudes to the Munich Agreement:

> The letter from The Scotsman (Source A) expresses a personal and private opinion but also a minority opinion, since the writer believes that Munich was wrong. Source B, on the other hand, defends the Munich Agreement as probably the best that could have been achieved at the time. It was written in 1940 when Britain was at war and two years after the events, so the writer knows that the Munich Agreement did not secure peace. In other words the writer of Source B has the advantage of hindsight – he knows what happened next in the story whereas the writer of Source A did not.

Then compare the content of the sources and their meaning:

> Source A states that "Britain and France have shown that they are not willing to fight for Czechoslovakia but they are willing to hand over her industry, property etc. to Hitler as it stands' and "Britain and France appear to have thrown Czechoslovakia to the wolves' meaning that Britain and France are prepared to buy peace at the price of giving Czech land and resources to an aggressive power.

> In Source B, on the other hand, Kennedy says 'Chamberlain was sincere in thinking that a great step had been taken towards healing one of Europe's fever sores' and that 'Munich was inevitable on the grounds of lack of armaments alone.' Kennedy believes that the treaties after World War I had left the Sudetenland as a source of future tension and that Chamberlain was right in his attempt to ease that tension. Kennedy also believed that Britain's military was not ready to fight a war.

This part of your answer makes a direct comparison and uses content and some recall to support your point. The use of the phrase 'on the other hand' makes it clear to a marker that you are comparing (which is what you are asked to do).

Now make clear you understand the difference in opinion:

> The writer of Source A believes that the Munich Agreement was wrong and that 'thousands of people will be shocked and humiliated'. But in Source B, the author believes that 'Most people in Britain felt, "It's not worth a war".'

When you finish your answer, sum up by clearly indicating that you know what was meant by Appeasement by identifying which source supported the policy and which source did not:

> In this case, the writer of Source A was very much opposed to the Munich Agreement and was therefore against Appeasement, while Kennedy accepts that Appeasement was a realistic policy and so supports Appeasement to an extent (another comparison point).

> Honesty check:
> If you didn't include these points do you now understand them? If not, use these gaps in your knowledge as points to revise or to ask your teacher/tutor about.

The End of Czechoslovakia, March 1939

Syllabus relevance

Intermediate 2:

> There is nothing mentioned in the syllabus about Czechoslovakia after the Munich Agreement but the background to the Polish crisis, which is in the syllabus, links to events in Czechoslovakia in 1939.

Higher:

> There will not be a specific source reference to events after Munich but the syllabus states 'The Fate of Czechoslovakia' as a section expected to be covered in the lead up to the declaration of war.

At a glance

In March 1939, Hitler tore up the promises made at Munich and invaded the western part of Czechoslovakia called Bohemia and Moravia (see map on page 88). Hitler's actions effectively destroyed any hopes that Appeasement might prevent war.

When Hitler gained the Sudetenland, the rest of Czechoslovakia was left defenceless. For many people, the settlement of the Czech crisis at Munich suggested that Europe could look forward to a 'Christmas of Peace'. In fact, Hitler's promise that he had 'no more territorial demands in Europe' only lasted six months.

When Hitler ordered the invasion of western Czechoslovakia in March 1939, the policy of Appeasement was discredited. Public opinion in Britain and France suddenly changed towards an acceptance that Hitler could only be stopped by force.

Other World Events in . . .

1939 Albert Einstein writes a letter to US President Franklin Roosevelt, alerting him to the possibility of using uranium to initiate a nuclear chain reaction, the fundamental process behind the atomic bomb.

The films *Gone With the Wind* and *The Wizard of Oz* are released.

Bob Kane creates the cartoon character 'Batman' for *DC Comics*.

In a speech to Parliament at the end of March 1939, Chamberlain seemed to admit that Appeasement had failed:

> 'Have we now to accept that Hitler will not stop and that he cannot be trusted to keep his promises? Must we now face the real possibility that only war will stop the spread of Nazi power? . . . Let me say now that Britain will help Poland if it is attacked by Germany.'

By April, Britain had made promises to protect Poland and Romania, Hitler's next likely targets in his move eastwards. A few weeks later, the British government began to prepare an army to fight in Europe. This was a major change in Britain's policy. But why should Hitler worry? He believed that Britain's promises meant nothing.

Section summary

In this section you should have learned that:
- Hitler broke the Munich Agreement in March 1939;
- the destruction of Czechoslovakia changed attitudes in Britain towards Appeasement.

These ideas are vital to an understanding of this section of the course. If you are unsure about them go back to your SOI. Use any gaps in your knowledge to your advantage. They will provide a focus for further revision or as questions to ask your teacher/tutor about.

Poland and the Final Steps to War, March to September 1939

Syllabus relevance
Intermediate 2:
>   Foreign Policy in practice – 'the Polish crisis and the declaration of war'

Higher:
>   'The Polish crisis and events leading up to the outbreak of war in September 1939'

At a glance
In March 1939, Britain promised to protect Poland against an attack from Germany. The promise to Poland marked the end of Appeasement, but at the time it seemed unlikely that Britain could do much to help Poland, especially when Hitler made an agreement with Russia. However, Hitler's attack on Poland in September 1939 led to the Second World War.

Why was there a Polish Crisis?
Poland was created at the end of World War I, partly from land taken from Germany and Russia. Look back at the map on page 59 to see how Polish land divided the bulk of Germany from a smaller part called East Prussia. That part of Poland was called the Polish Corridor and contained mostly German-speaking people. Naturally, Hitler complained about the Polish Corridor and the treatment of Germans in this region was Hitler's excuse for pressurising Poland in 1939.

Why was Russia important to the Polish Crisis?
Britain hoped that an alliance with Russia would make Hitler stop because an attack on Poland would risk a war with Russia. But would Russia be prepared to fight for Poland? The leader of Russia, Joseph Stalin, was worried because Russia was not ready to fight. Stalin was also annoyed with and suspicious of Britain and France. He had not been invited to the Munich conference and, in April 1939, Russia's suggestion of an alliance with Britain was rejected. The problem was that Britain was reluctant to make an agreement with communist Russia while Poland, an old enemy of Russia, would not allow Russian soldiers into Poland. The result was that by the summer of 1939 no deal between Poland, Britain and Russia had been made.

The Nazi-Soviet Non-Aggression Pact
The agreement signed between Hitler and Stalin on August 23, 1939 shocked the world because each side was supposed to be the sworn enemy of the other. It was called the Nazi-Soviet Non-Aggression Pact – or sometimes the Molotov-Ribbentrop Agreement after the Russian and German negotiators.

The agreement stated that Germany and Russia would not fight each other. There was also a secret part to the pact. In private, Stalin and Hitler had agreed to divide up Poland between them! The immediate consequence of the agreement was that Germany was free to attack Poland since Russia would not fight to protect it. One week after the Nazi-Soviet agreement was signed, Nazi tanks rolled into Poland on September 1, 1939.

When Hitler invaded Poland, he believed he would have a short, easy war. Russia was now on his side and although Britain had promised to fight for Poland, there was no way Britain could send help across Europe. Hitler was sure that Britain would give in as she always had before.

Hitler was surprised when Chamberlain said that Britain would declare war if German troops did not retreat from Poland. On the morning of September 3, 1939 Chamberlain spoke on radio to the British people to tell them that 'this country is at war with Germany' since the German invasion of Poland was continuing.

BEWARE!

By September 3, 1939 Britain was at war with Germany, yet year after year in exam questions that ask about British policy towards Germany in the late 1930s – or even worse, 'up to and including 1939' – candidates still write only about Appeasement. Remember that British policy towards Germany changed in the late 1930s. How else can you explain the declaration of war! This was not Appeasement in action.

Section summary

In this section you should have learned that:

- Britain's promise to protect Poland marked the end of Appeasement;
- Britain's hopes of making a deal with Russia ended when Russia made a surprise deal with Germany;
- Hitler's attack on Poland led to the Second World War.

These ideas are vital to an understanding of this section of the course. If you are unsure about them go back to your SOI. Use any gaps in your knowledge to your advantage. They will provide a focus for further revision or as questions to ask your teacher/tutor about.

Practise your skills

Remember, in Paper 2 all the questions will be based around the sources in the exam paper. However, as you have seen at the beginning of these assessments, it is possible to be asked about events just before and after the content of the sources. The direct source content can only include events up to the Munich Agreement, but a source produced at the time of the Munich Agreement may well refer to what they expect to happen next. Likewise, a secondary source could look at the consequences of Munich. In other words, you can expect questions which will test your knowledge of events after Munich up to the outbreak of war in September 1939. That's what you have to deal with in the next question.

Activity

To what extent did subsequent events confirm this prediction of The Economist?

From *The Economist*, 8 October 1938

> There cannot be any doubt that peace has been purchased at the price of the overwhelming defeat of international principles. . . The lesson of the last three weeks is that potential aggressors will get what they want, whether it is just or unjust, if they bully, bluff and threaten.

- First of all, are you sure what the word 'subsequent' means? If not, find out.
- Secondly, the question requires you to identify the prediction of *The Economist* and match that against what happened after Munich. Consider in your answer – did the bullies get what they want? Did the bullies continue to bluff and threaten? Did Appeasement continue?
- You must combine an answer to this question with demonstrating your knowledge of events between October 1938 and September 1939.

Honesty check:

If you find it difficult to write an answer based around these points use that to your advantage by asking your teacher/tutor to help you work on those skills.

Why Appeasement?

Syllabus relevance

Intermediate 2:
'The policy of Appeasement and reasons for its adoption . . .'
Higher:
Although there is no specific reference in the syllabus to 'reasons for Appeasement', you may well find a question that asks why Britain adopted a policy of Appeasement in the 1930s.

At a glance

A traditional view of Appeasement is that it was a policy of cowardice, but recent research has shown there were many reasons why the British government adopted it.

When explaining why Britain adopted a policy of Appeasement, try to avoid oversimplification by claiming that Appeasement was a policy of fear and cowardice and that its only aim was to avoid war.

In any answer to the question of why Britain adopted a policy of Appeasement you must think of the various pressures that were on the politicians.

In summary these pressures were:

- Public opinion/fear of another war
  The government had to listen to popular opinion since all adults, male and female, now had the right to vote. Without doubt, the British public wanted peace. They feared a repeat of the last war (those who had fought now had sons of military age) and they feared a new war involving gas bombing of cities. (This had been graphically illustrated in the 1936 film *Things to Come*, in which British cities are destroyed by bombing and the civilian population suffers gas attacks. The movie predicted the war would start in 1940 and would destroy civilisation.)

- Versailles was too harsh
  By the mid 1930s, the public and politicians alike believed that some of Hitler's complaints were justified and that Hitler had legitimate grievances. After one part of the treaty was changed, why resist others?

- Hitler was a reasonable man who could be talked to
  Chamberlain believed that Hitler was making extreme statements only to gain publicity and that he was essentially a reasonable man who would choose negotiation rather than conflict.

- The Empire was Britain's main concern
  Any war in Europe involving Britain would threaten the security of her Empire. During the 1930s, the British Empire was threatened by Italy and Japan. Britain also had to control trouble in India, the Middle East (20,000 British troops were needed there in 1938) and in Ireland. In short, the Empire came first. Appeasement – keeping out of European conflicts – therefore made sense.

- The Empire might split up
  In 1937 South Africa had told Britain that, if Britain fought a war over Czechoslovakia, South Africa would not get involved. If that happened, how long would it be before New Zealand, Australia and Canada said a European war was not their problem? If that happened, Britain would be severely weakened.

- Britain had no reliable allies
  France was politically divided, Italy and Germany were allies with each other and, by late 1939, Russia was also allied to Hitler. In 1938, the United States was firmly isolationist and Chamberlain believed that he could expect no help from America. In a private letter to his sister, he had written, 'You can count on the Americans for nothing but words.'

- Too weak to fight – Britain needed time to rearm
  The heads of Britain's armed forces – the Chiefs of Staff – had consistently warned Chamberlain that Britain was too weak to fight. At the same time, Hitler's propaganda encouraged Britain and France to believe that Nazi forces were stronger than they really were.

- Fear of Communism
  A common saying at the time was 'better Hitlerism than Communism' and many people wondered what the point of fighting Nazism was, if the result would be that Communists came to power in European countries.

So, would you have appeased in the 1930s or not? Do you think it was a policy of cowardice and foolishness? Or was Appeasement a rational response to the situation confronting Britain in the 1930s?

Section summary

In this section you should have learned that:

- in the years after World War Two, the policy of Appeasement was condemned as a policy of stupidity and cowardice;
- since the late 1960s, many more reasons have emerged to explain why Britain adopted Appeasement.

These ideas are vital to an understanding of this section of the course. If you are unsure about them go back to your SOI. Use any gaps in your knowledge to your advantage. They will provide a focus for further revision or as questions to ask your teacher/tutor about.

Chapter Index

Appendices

Biographies
Possible Careers
Bibliography
Website Addresses

Biographies

Napoleon Bonaparte

b. August 15, 1759, d. May 5, 1821

Napoleon rose to fame during the French Revolution (1789–1799). As commander of the French Revolutionary armies he seized political power and proclaimed himself Emperor of France in 1804. His military victories extended French rule over much of Europe. Although Napoleon was seen as a terrible threat by the old aristocratic rulers of Europe, the Liberals and Nationalists at first saw him as the person who could bring about change. After all, the slogan of the French Revolution was *Liberté, Egalité, Fraternité* (Liberty, Equality, Fraternity).

However, it soon became clear that Napoleon was not going to free Europe; but rather, he enslaved it by strictly controlling his conquered territories. In 1815, Napoleon's ambitions were finally crushed by defeat at the Battle of Waterloo at the hands of British, Dutch and Prussian soldiers, led by the Duke of Wellington. About one million French soldiers had died in battle or as a result of disease during the 11 years of the Napoleonic Wars. In hindsight, Napoleon upset the European political balance of power. The ideals of the French Revolution were at the root of most of Europe's political changes in the 19th century but, when Napoleon died in 1821, it looked as if the Old Order was back in control.

Prince Klemens von Metternich

b. May 15, 1773, d. June 11, 1859

Metterich was born in Koblenz in the Rhineland. Between 1809 and 1848, he was Foreign Minister of the Austrian Empire and Chancellor between 1821 and 1848. He believed that strong government was needed to prevent revolution. He was opposed to Nationalism and Liberalism, ideologies which he believed threatened the Austrian Empire. He also tried to maintain the power of Austria at the expense of Prussia.

Metternich helped defeat Napoleon, for which he was made a prince in 1813. He was a major influence in creating the German Confederation under an Austrian presidency in 1815. Metternich became a symbol of the Old Order which stood against change. He was forced from power by the Revolutions of 1848, after which he fled to Britain. Just before he died, he said, 'I was a rock of order'.

Frederick William IV

b. October 15, 1795, d. January 2, 1861

Frederick William became King of Prussia in 1840. During the revolution of 1848 in Prussia, he at first tried to crush the risings but changed his mind as he realised he could become a possible leader of a united Germany. However, by 1849, Frederick William had changed his mind again and rejected a request from the Frankfurt Parliament that he should be king of a united Germany. He believed that monarchs were created by God. He did not believe that a parliament had a right to choose a king and so rejected the Frankfurt Parliament's invitation to be King of Germany. He is said to have called the offer 'a crown from the gutter'. In 1850, Frederick William was forced to give up his hopes of leading a united Germany when Austria forced him to accept the Treaty of Olmutz. In 1857, Frederick William suffered a stroke and was forced to resign his administration to his brother who, from 1858, acted as regent until his accession, as Wilhelm I, on Frederick William's death.

Otto von Bismarck

b. April 1, 1815, d. July 30, 1898

Bismarck's family were landowners in Prussia and in the Revolutions of 1848, Bismarck made it clear he was against change and even supported the continued Austrian leadership in Germany. In the 1850s, he was Prussian Minister to the German Confederation in Frankfurt and worked to secure Prussian interests, without regard to consistent policy or ideology. After a short time representing Prussia in St. Petersburg and Paris, he was asked to become Minister-President and Foreign Minister for the Prussian King, Wilhelm I.

Bismarck is remembered as the man who brought about German unification between 1864 and 1871, mainly as a result of three wars against Denmark, Austria and France. These wars demonstrated Bismarck's diplomacy, his ability to plan and also his ability to make use of chance occurrences and manipulate events to his advantage.

His diplomacy brought victorious wars against Denmark (over Schleswig-Holstein in 1864) and against Austria (the Seven Weeks War of 1866). The North German Confederation was formed in 1867 under Prussian control. In 1870, Bismarck's backing of a Hohenzollern prince as candidate for the Spanish throne led to war against France. After France was defeated, the German Empire was proclaimed at Versailles on January 18, 1871, and Bismarck became German Chancellor.

As Chancellor, Bismarck's foreign policy was directed at maintaining and strengthening the power of the German Empire. To that end, he established a network of alliances called the Bismarck system, his main concern being to isolate France so that she would never achieve her dream of revenge against Germany.

Domestically, Bismarck was concerned with maintaining Prussian authority over the newly united Germany. The new constitution, although seemingly democratic, merely disguised the power held by Bismarck through his influence over the Kaiser. Bismarck was also concerned with keeping Germany safe from internal threats to its unity. In the 1870s, Bismarck considered Catholics to be a threat and spent many years trying to undermine Catholic influence in Germany. However, when Bismarck found Socialism to be a bigger threat he abandoned his anti-Catholic policies (the *Kulturkampf*) and began a series of policies aimed at weakening the attraction of Socialism. In 1890, the new Kaiser disagreed with Bismarck over his policies towards the Socialists and so Bismarck resigned.

In the short term, Bismarck's policies kept his new, young creation – Germany – stable, but in the longer term he kept alive the power of the landed aristocracy in Germany and, under Wilhelm II, Bismarck's alliance system contributed directly to World War I and the collapse of the German Empire.

Paul von Hindenburg

b. October 2, 1847, d. August 2, 1934

Hindenburg served as a German field marshal in World War I. In the mid 1920s, the new democratic Weimar Republic had few strong supporters. Most people were disillusioned with democratic party politics and the problems facing Germany as a result of losing World War I. Some historians explain Hindenburg's victory in the Presidential election of 1925 by claiming that, for many Germans, Hindenburg represented stability, a living reminder of the good old days of pre-war Germany and even a substitute Kaiser. Hindenburg was re-elected as President in 1932 but by this time he was an old man, easily under the influence of politicians who hoped to use his presidential powers for their own ends.

Hindenburg hated Hitler, but was persuaded to appoint him Chancellor. Following Hindenburg's death in 1934, democracy in Germany was all but dead as Hitler established his dictatorship.

Kaiser Wilhelm II

b. January 27, 1859, d. June 4, 1941

Wilhelm was King of Prussia and Kaiser of Germany from 1888 until 1918. His decision-making was inconsistent and he has been blamed for leading Germany into war in 1914. Wilhelm was against Liberalism and the spread of democracy in Germany. He believed in the divine right of kings to rule and was against any form of control by parliamentary government. Wilhelm wanted to 'rule as well as reign'. He disagreed with Bismarck's policies and, as a result, Bismarck resigned in 1890, leaving Wilhelm free to increase his own authority. Wilhelm listened closely to military advisers and industrialists who wanted to increase Germany's influence in the world. His foreign policy destabilised Europe before 1914 with warlike speeches, the building of a large navy and expansion of the German army. These actions worried Britain and France and increased tension in Europe. Wilhelm also offended Russia by breaking earlier agreements and supporting Austro-Hungarian expansion in the Balkans. As a result of Wilhelm's actions Britain, France and Russia made agreements aimed at blocking German expansion.

Wilhelm led Germany to defeat in World War I and just before Germany surrendered he abdicated. Two million German soldiers were dead. Wilhelm spent the rest of his life in Holland where he died in 1941.

Arthur Neville Chamberlain

b. March 18, 1869, d. November 9, 1940

Between 1931 and 1937, Chamberlain served in the British National Government as Chancellor of the Exchequer. As Prime Minister from 1937 to 1940, he will always be linked to the policy of Appeasement. Critics of Chamberlain argue that his failure to stand up against Nazi aggression encouraged Hitler to make even more demands; whilst his supporters believe that appeasement was a sensible policy at the time, given Britain's relative weakness and public opinion which was strongly anti-war until 1939. During the Czechoslovakian crisis of 1938, Chamberlain met Hitler several times and he returned from the Munich Conference claiming to have secured 'peace for our time.' Although Chamberlain was cheered as a hero in October 1938, he was discredited when Hitler broke his promises the following year. He resigned as Prime Minister in 1940 and died a few weeks later.

Joseph Stalin

b. December 21, 1879. d. March 5, 1953

In 1917, the Bolshevik Revolution turned Russia into a Communist state under the leadership of Vladimir Ilyich Ulyanov (Lenin). Stalin was an important member of the Bolshevik party (which had split from the Russian Social Democratic Workers' Party in 1903 and became known as the Communist Party in 1918). After Lenin's death in 1924, Stalin used his control of the party organisation to murder and otherwise remove his opponents. By the end of 1929, Stalin was the unchallenged dictator of the USSR, as Communist Russia was now known.

Stalin knew he had to modernise Russian agriculture and industry or its enemies would crush it. The programme to make Russian agriculture more efficient was known as Collectivisation and Stalin's five-year plans set targets for Russian industry to meet.

During the 1930s, Stalin knew Nazi Germany had ambitions to take over Russia and for that reason he pushed even harder to modernise the country. But Stalin used terror to maintain his control. The secret police imprisoned and/or murdered large sections of any group that Stalin considered a potential threat to his power. Deaths have been estimated in the millions. After attempts in the late 1930s to reach agreements with Britain and France had failed, Stalin shocked the world by making a non-aggression pact with Hitler. The agreement bought Stalin some time, but in June 1941 Nazi Germany attacked the USSR.

By 1945, Stalin was at the height of his power. He was seen by many Russians as the man who saved the USSR from the Nazis and, as the Red Army spread over Eastern Europe after the collapse of Nazi Germany, Stalin established communist puppet governments in Eastern Europe. Stalin died in 1953, but his legacy of a divided Europe and a Cold War lived on long after his death, alongside the question of exactly how many people were murdered on his orders – estimates range from 20 to 50 million people over a period of thirty years.

Benito Mussolini

b. July 29, 1883, d. April 28, 1945

Founder of Italian Fascism and Premier (1922–43) of Italy, Mussolini ruled Italy as dictator from 1925. In 1912, Mussolini was the editor of the Socialist Party newspaper *Avanti!* and when World War I began in 1914 was opposed to Italy's involvement. However, he changed his mind and was expelled from the Socialist Party. He served in the army until he was wounded in 1917. In 1919, Mussolini and others founded the *Fasci di Combattimento*, a new nationalist party, in Milan. This Fascist movement was against Socialists, Communists and Democrats. By 1925–26, he had created a single-party, totalitarian dictatorship. Mussolini was known as *Il Duce* ('the leader').

In the mid 1930s, Mussolini adopted an aggressive foreign policy, conquering Abyssinia in 1936 and helping General Franco win the Spanish Civil War. Also in 1936, Mussolini and Hitler became allies, a friendship which led to the Rome-Berlin Axis and which fundamentally altered the balance of power in Europe in favour of these two dictators. Mussolini passed laws which discriminated against Italy's Jews and did nothing to stop German troops who captured these people from their homes and took them to concentration camps in Germany. Once Britain realised Mussolini could not be relied on as an ally against Hitler, it was almost inevitable that the policy of appeasement would continue. Italy joined World War Two against Britain in 1940, but, by 1943, had lost all support in Italy and was imprisoned. However, he was freed by a daring German rescue only two months later and was made head of a Fascist puppet government in North Italy. In 1945, while trying to escape advancing allied armies, Mussolini and his mistress were captured by Italian partisans who shot them both. Their bodies were brought to Milan and hung upside down in a public square before being buried in an unmarked grave.

Although Mussolini had been popular with most Italians until the late 1930s, he lost their support when he took them into an unpopular war which Italy was not ready to fight.

Adolf Hitler

b. April 20, 1889, d. April 30, 1945

Hitler was born in Austria. However, he fought in the German army during World War One and was awarded the Iron Cross, First Class for bravery. Hitler hated the Treaty of Versailles, which represented German humiliation after defeat in World War I. By 1920, he was a member of a right-wing party which came to be known as the Nazis. After an attempt to seize power in Germany in 1923, Hitler served a short prison sentence but then faded from the political scene until the economic crisis of 1929. Rocketing unemployment made people listen to the extreme messages of the Nazis. Hitler offered hope, pride, food and work to the German people. His ideas were outlined in his book *Mein Kampf* ('My Struggle') written during his imprisonment, in which he claimed Jews and Communists were the enemies of Germany. He promised to restore German power and claimed that the pure German people – whom he inaccurately described as 'Aryans' – were a master race who had a right to dominate Europe. By early 1933, Hitler had become Chancellor of Germany and a few months later he was its dictator.

In Germany, Hitler established a totalitarian dictatorship. The Nazi party was the only political party allowed. Through a combination of popular policies and fear, force and propaganda, Hitler and the Nazis established a stranglehold over Germany. During the 1930s, for 'good' Germans (ie those who supported the Nazis and fitted in with Nazi ideals) life seemed to get better with jobs, food and popular leisure activities all organised by the state. For those people the Nazis disapproved of, especially the Jews, life got worse. Secret police spied on the population and concentration camps were used to imprison any opposition. Nazi Germany was a Police State. The Nazis made the laws, enforced the laws and judged who was guilty or innocent.

The ideology of Nazism, created by Hitler, led to the Holocaust in which six million Jewish men, women and children were captured without trial, having committed no crimes; deported in cattle trains and held in concentration camps where they were starved, tortured and murdered. A further five million people: those with physical and mental disabilities, homosexuals, gypsies, political objectors and other opponents suffered as a result of Nazi ideology and were also abused and murdered.

Hitler's foreign policy was a combination of expansion and the uniting of all German-speaking people into a Greater Germany and aimed for the destruction of the Treaty of Versailles. Between 1935 and 1939, Hitler's breaking of treaty agreements and aggression was met with appeasement. Realising he was not going to meet forceful opposition, Hitler demanded, and got, more and more concessions from his former enemies, Britain and France. It was not until September 1939, when Nazi Germany invaded Poland, that Britain and France declared war on Germany, thereby starting World War Two. The war ended in 1945, just days after Hitler committed suicide in the ruins of Berlin.

Possible Careers

Why study History?

The Intermediate 2 and Higher History course supported in this book provides you with two main assets which can be used to your advantage in your next steps after leaving school.

The first asset is a body of knowledge about the background and roots of modern Britain and another major player in the world today, usually Germany or the United States.

The second asset is probably even more important. It is the very marketable skills you have acquired during the course:

- The ability to present a structured argument, weighing up evidence, looking at several sides to an argument and making a considered and balanced decision. Whether you work in a court of law or justifying your decision on what product to buy for a company you work for, these are skills you will use all your working life.

- The ability to analyse evidence, compare it with differing viewpoints and identify bias. Being able to weigh up opinions and spot how much or how little they represent widely held viewpoints is vital in many areas where dealing with the public is a prime concern.

Careers

The following list is not complete. Its aim is to give you some ideas where the skills and content you have learned in this History course will come in useful.

- advertising
- architecture
- archivist
- armed forces
- business
- civil service
- primary or secondary teaching
- heritage industry
- historian
- journalism
- law
- librarianship
- marketing
- politics, local and national
- public relations
- publishing
- researcher
- tourism and leisure
- working towards a degree.

Bibliography

At the end of each section below, there are a number of references to articles published in the magazine *Modern History Review*. The first number refers to the volume, the second to the issue (there are four issues to each volume).

General Histories of Germany

Ronald Cameron, Charles Robertson & Christine Henderson, *The Growth of Nationalism: Germany and Italy, 1815–1939*
(Pulse Publications, ISBN: 0948766158)
Gordon A Craig, *Germany, 1866–1945*
(Oxford Paperbacks, ISBN: 0192851012)
Golo Mann, *The History of Germany since 1789*
(Chatto and Windus, ISBN: 0701113464)
Modern History Review articles: 2/4; 11/1

Bismarck and the Unification of Germany

John Breuilly, *Austria, Prussia and Germany, 1806–1871*
(Longman, ISBN: 0582437393)
Alan Farmer & Andrina Stiles, *The Unification of Germany, 1815–90*
(Hodder & Stoughton Educational, ISBN: 0340781424)
Michael Gorman, *The Unification of Germany*
(Cambridge University Press, ISBN: 521317304)
David Hargreaves, *Bismarck and German Unification*
(Palgrave MacMillan, ISBN: 0333537750)
ARC Hewison, *Bismarck and the Unification of Germany*
(Edward Arnold, ISBN: 0713116064)
Otto Pflanze, *Bismarck and the Development of Germany, Volume 1: The Period of Unification, 1815–1871*
(Princeton University Press, ISBN: 0691055874)
AJP Taylor, *Bismarck*
(Penguin, ISBN: 0141391170)
David G Williamson, *Bismarck and Germany, 1862–1890*
(Longman, ISBN: 0582293219)
Modern History Review articles: 7/3; 8/2; 11/3; 12/1; 12/3; 13/2; 13/3

The German Empire, 1871–1918

Lynn Abrams, *Bismarck and the German Empire, 1871–1918*
(Routledge, ISBN: 0415077818)
Erich Eyck, *Bismarck and the German Empire*
(W W Norton & Company, ISBN: 0393002357)
John van der Kiste, *Kaiser Wilhelm II*
(Sutton Publishing, ISBN: 0750927364)
Ian Porter & Ian Armour, *Imperial Germany, 1890–1918*
(Longman, ISBN: 0582034965)
James Retallack, *Germany in the Age of Kaiser Wilhelm II*
(Palgrave Macmillan, ISBN: 0333592425)
Modern History Review articles: 2/2; 7/1; 8/2; 9/3; 10/4; 11/3; 11/4; 12/3

The Weimar Republic, Hitler and the Third Reich

Henry Ashby Turner, Jr, *Hitler's Thirty Days to Power*
(Bloomsbury, ISBN: 0747531714)
Richard Bessel, *Life in the Third Reich*
(Oxford Paperbacks, ISBN: 0192802100)
Andrew Boxer, *Hitler's Domestic Policy*
(Collins Educational, ISBN: 000327117x)
Michael Burleigh, *The Third Reich: A New History*
(Pan, ISBN: 0330487574)
Martin Collier & Philip Pedley, *Heinemann Advanced History: Germany, 1919–45*
(Heinemann Educational Secondary Division, ISBN: 043527216)
Richard Grunberger, *The 12-Year Reich: A Social History of Nazi Germany, 1933–1945*
(Da Capo Press, ISBN: 0306806606)

John Hiden, *The Weimar Republic*
 (Longman, ISBN: 0582287065)
Ian Kershaw, *Hitler, 1889–1936: Hubris*
 (Penguin Books, ISBN: 0140133631)
Ian Kershaw, *Hitler, 1936–1945: Nemesis*
 (Penguin Books, ISBN: 0140272399)
Ian Kershaw, *The Nazi Dictatorship*
 (Arnold, ISBN: 0340760281)
Claudia Koonz, *Mothers in the Fatherland: Women, the Family and Nazi Politics*
 (St Martin's Press, ISBN: 0312022565)
Guido Knopp, *Hitler's Children*
 (Sutton Publishing, ISBN: 0750927321)
Christian Leitz, *The Third Reich*
 (Blackwell Publishers, ISBN: 0631207007)
Samuel W Mitcham, *Why Hitler? The Genesis of the Nazi Reich*
 (Praeger Publishers, ISBN: 0275954854)
Jeremy Noakes & Geoffrey Pridham, *Nazism, 1919–1945*
 (University of Exeter Press, Four Volumes)
William L Shirer, *The Rise and Fall of the Third Reich*
 (Arrow, ISBN: 0099421763)
Albert Speer, *Inside the Third Reich*
 (Phoenix Mass Market Paperback, ISBN: 1857992180)
David G Williamson, *The Third Reich*
 (Longman, ISBN: 0582368839)
Modern History Review articles (The Weimar Republic): 8/1; 9/1; 9/2; 10/1; 11/1; 12/2

Modern History Review articles (Nazi Germany): 6/4; 7/1; 7/4; 9/2; 11/4; 12/3; 13/1; 13/3

Appeasement and the Road to War

Andrew Boxer, *Questions in History: Appeasement*
 (Collins Educational, ISBN: 000327117x)
Piers Brendon, *The Dark Valley: A Panorama of the 1930s*
 (Pimlico, ISBN: 0712667148)
Ronald Cameron, *Appeasement and the Road to War*
 (Pulse Publications, ISBN: 0948766107)
Graham Darby, *Hitler, Appeasement and the Road to War, 1933–41*
 (Hodder & Stoughton Educational, ISBN: 0340746971)
Erik Goldstein, *The First World War Peace Settlements*
 (Longman, ISBN: 0582311454)
Frank McDonough, *Hitler, Chamberlain and Appeasement*
 (Cambridge University Press, ISBN: 0521000483)
Frank McDonough, *Neville Chamberlain, Appeasement and the Road to War*
 (Manchester University Press, ISBN: 071904832x)
Alastair Parker, *Chamberlain and Appeasement*
 (Palgrave MacMillan, ISBN: 0333417135)
RJ Overy, *The Inter-War Crisis, 1919–1939*
 (Longman, ISBN: 0582353793)
RJ Overy, *The Origins of the Second World War*
 (Longman, ISBN: 0582290856)
RJ Overy & Andrew Wheatcroft, *The Road to War*
 (Penguin, ISBN: 014028530x)
Keith Robbins, *Appeasement*
 (Blackwell Publishers, ISBN: 0631203265)
AJP Taylor, *The Origins of the Second World War*
 (Penguin, ISBN: 014013672x)
Ted Townley, *Hitler and the Road to War*
 (Collins Educational, ISBN: 0003271188)
Robert Wolfson & John Laver, *Years of Change*
 (Hodder & Stoughton Educational, ISBN: 0340775262)
Modern History Review articles: 1/2; 1/3; 3/2; 4/1; 5/4; 6/3; 10/3; 12/4; 13/4

The Holocaust

Yehuda Bauer, *Rethinking the Holocaust*
    (Yale Nota Bene, ISBN: 0300093004)
Martin Gilbert, *The Holocaust*
    (HarperCollins, ISBN: 0006371949)
Thomas Keneally, *Schindler's List*
    (Hodder & Stoughton, ISBN: 0340606517)
Guido Knopp, *Hitler's Holocaust*
    (Sutton Publishing, ISBN: 0750927003)
Modern History Review articles: 3/2; 10/2; 11/1; 12/1; 12/2

Website Addresses

Unlike conventionally published books, most websites are not subjected to a process of quality review. Consequently, the usefulness of historical material available on the internet is varied, and many sites contain misleading and inaccurate information.

Web resources should not be regarded as a full substitute for your textbooks and other history books, but the selected sites below may be of some use.

Although these links were correct at the time of printing, due to the dynamic nature of the internet Leckie & Leckie can not be held responsible for their content.

General History Websites of Value

http://www.activehistory.co.uk

Although designed for students studying for their GCSEs and A-Levels, this site has excellent interactive resources for teachers and students on such topics as 'Germany in the era of Bismarck' and the Weimar Republic. It even provides you with a chance to interview Hitler!

http://www.bbc.co.uk/history

BBC History's homepage. You will find a lot of information here, most of it in summary form. The site is constantly updated to complement history programmes on BBC1 and BBC2.

http://www.channel4.com/history/

Not as broad as the BBC's history site, but there are nevertheless some interesting topics to be found here, most of which complement Channel 4's history programming.

http://www.eb.com/

The Encyclopedia Britannica Online is vast in scope.

http://www.fordham.edu/halsall/mod/modsbook.html

The Internet Modern History Sourcebook is an exhaustive series of links to primary documents about almost every conceivable aspect of Modern History.

http://www.history-ontheweb.co.uk/

A site of free resources for Modern History students and teachers.

http://www.historychannel.com/

The homepage of The History Channel has an American bias and does not go into great depth, but nevertheless provides good summaries of the events discussed in this book.

http://www.pbs.org/history/

Online support for the numerous history programs produced by the American PBS channel. Although the emphasis is on American history, there are also some good resources for the topics studied in this book.

http://www.spartacus.schoolnet.co.uk/

The Spartacus Educational website provides a series of history encyclopedias. Titles currently include British History: 1750–1960; The United States: 1840–1980; First World War; Second World War; Russia: 1860–1945; Germany: 1900–1945; and France: 1900–1945. Entries usually include a narrative, illustrations and primary sources.

http://library.kent.ac.uk/cartoons/

The Centre for the Study of Cartoons and Caricatures allows you to to search for more cartoons dealing with events in this book, as well as other periods of history.

http://www.yale.edu/lawweb/avalon/avalon.htm

The Avalon Project at Yale University provides numerous primary documents. Collections include 'From Versailles to NATO', 'The League of Nations' and 'Nazi-Soviet Relations, 1939–1941'.

General Histories of Germany

http://mars.vnet.wnec.edu/~grempel/courses/germany/lectures.html

A very thorough collection of lectures from a university history course in America. You will find a vast amount of information in the 52 lectures included on this website. However, of particular interest are lectures 4–35 (Prussian Tradition–Defeat and Rebirth).

Bismarck and the Unification of Germany

http://www.geocities.com/Athens/Rhodes/6916/unification.htm

A good summary of the history of German Unification.

http://www.ohiou.edu/~Chastain/index.htm

An Encyclopedia of the 1848 Revolutions, maintained by the University of Ohio.

The German Empire, 1871–1918

http://mars.wnec.edu/~grempel/courses/ww1/lectures.html

Detailed lecture notes on the First World War.

The Weimar Republic, Hitler and the Third Reich

http://www.calvin.edu/academic/cas/gpa/

A look at the use of propaganda in the Third Reich.

http://www.historyplace.com/worldwar2/riseofhitler/index.htm

Detailed notes on the rise of Hitler.

http://mars.wnec.edu/~grempel/courses/hitler/lectures.html

Detailed lecture notes discussing Hitler and Nazi Germany.

http://www.thecorner.org/hists/total/n-german.htm

A good summary of the rise of Hitler and the establishment of Nazi Germany.

http://www.ushmm.org/wlc/en/index.php?ModuleId=10005680

This site looks in detail at the 1936 Berlin Olympics and explores such topics as 'Race Hygiene' and 'Sport as Military Training'.

Appeasement and the Road to War

http://www.bbc.co.uk/history/war/wwtwo/churchill_gathering_storm_01.shtml

Discusses if Winston Churchill has rewritten the history books to portray himself as a foreign policy visionary during the time of Appeasement.

http://mars.wnec.edu/~grempel/courses/ww2/lectures.html

Detailed lecture notes on the Second World War.

http://www.spartacus.schoolnet.co.uk/2WWevents.htm

A fully cross-referenced site, dealing with both the approach and course of the Second World War.

The Holocaust

http://www.annefrank.eril.net/

An online resource for the study of Anne Frank and the Holocaust.

http://www.het.org.uk/

The Holocaust Educational Trust promotes research into the Holocaust and its relevance today.

http://www.ushmm.org/

The United States Holocaust Memorial Museum website.

http://www.wiesenthal.com/

The Simon Wiesenthal Center is dedicated to preserving the memory of the Holocaust by fostering tolerance and understanding through community involvement, educational outreach and social action. Its website includes an extensive section aimed for both teachers and students of the Holocaust.